'For many in Christian ministry, the deat[h] ...
challenge. This book provides important ...
rounding such a tragedy, and a wealth of helpful advice on how best to respond to those issues. The author's expertise, gained over many years in his demanding role as chaplain to a children's hospital, has been distilled into a very readable handbook. Combining pastoral sensitivity with a well reasoned theological perspective, Paul Nash has written a valuable guide for all involved with the world of dying children today.'

Derek Fraser, Chair of the UK Board for Healthcare Chaplaincy

'*Supporting Dying Children and their Families* is written with sensitivity, compassion and deep insight into the unique loss which parents experience when their child is dying or has died. Chaplaincy teams and all those involved in pastoral and spiritual support will find a wealth of opportunities to reflect on their practice in ways that complement the care they give to bereaved families, whatever the circumstances of the child's death.'

Erica Brown, author and Vice President of Acorns Children's Hospice

'There is a wealth of information in this handbook, drawn from many different perspectives. Especially moving are the contributions from parents of children and young people who have died. It is a resource to dip into, reflect on and return to many times for those of us who care for families as we journey alongside them.'

Helen Jesty, Chaplain of Naomi House, near Winchester

'Supporting a family with a dying child is a "nightmare scenario" for many professionals in pastoral roles. Paul Nash offers us an accessible and comprehensive guidebook to supporting such families, which is deeply grounded in pastoral experience and can only serve to improve professional practice.'

Mark Birch, Chaplain of Helen and Douglas House, Oxford

'Combining immensely moving stories of dying children and their families with deep theological reflection, Paul Nash has created a book that gives practical advice and provides a theological framework for those who minister to and support dying children and their families, and I commend it.'

Michael Perham, Chair of the Hospital Chaplaincies Council, 2004–10

'As a patron of the UK's leading children's cancer charity, I know the anguish a child's death causes and the vital importance of caring support for bereaved families. It's why I believe *Supporting Dying Children and their Families* is very welcome. Through a mix of practical advice, spiritual guidance and real-life stories, together with the views of medical staff, this handbook will help Christian ministers and others provide the support that parents and families need.'

Cherie Blair, Patron of CLIC Sargent

The Revd Paul Nash is Senior Chaplain at Birmingham Children's Hospital and a co-founder and convener of the Paediatric Chaplaincy Network for Great Britain and Ireland. He is also a project leader for Red Balloon Resources (for multi-faith paediatric health, palliative and bereavement care, support and training) and a tutor at the Midlands Centre for Youth Ministry. His first ministry experience was with Youth for Christ, and when he left to be ordained he was part of the leadership team. He is involved in a number of community and church projects as well as chaplaincy work. He was the initiator of the Grove Youth Series and has written *What Theology for Youth Work?* (Grove, 2007). He and his wife Sally are the authors of *Tools for Reflective Ministry* (SPCK, 2009) and (with Jo Pimlott) *Skills for Collaborative Ministry* (SPCK, 2008).

SPCK Library of Ministry

COMMUNITY AND MINISTRY: AN INTRODUCTION TO COMMUNITY DEVELOPMENT IN A CHRISTIAN CONTEXT
Paul Ballard and Lesley Husselbee

PIONEER MINISTRY AND FRESH EXPRESSIONS OF CHURCH
Angela Shier-Jones

READER MINISTRY EXPLORED
Cathy Rowling and Paula Gooder

SKILLS FOR COLLABORATIVE MINISTRY
Sally Nash, Jo Pimlott and Paul Nash

SUPPORTING DYING CHILDREN AND THEIR FAMILIES: A HANDBOOK FOR CHRISTIAN MINISTRY
Paul Nash

SUPPORTING NEW MINISTERS IN THE LOCAL CHURCH: A HANDBOOK
Keith Lamdin and David Tilley

TOOLS FOR REFLECTIVE MINISTRY
Sally Nash and Paul Nash

SUPPORTING DYING CHILDREN AND THEIR FAMILIES

A handbook for Christian ministry

SPCK Library of Ministry

PAUL NASH

First published in Great Britain in 2011

Society for Promoting Christian Knowledge
36 Causton Street
London SW1P 4ST
www.spckpublishing.co.uk

British Library Cataloguing-in-Publication Data
A catalogue record for this book is available from the British Library

ISBN 978-0-281-06005-4

1 3 5 7 9 10 8 6 4 2

Typeset by Graphicraft Ltd, Hong Kong
Printed in Great Britain by MPG Books Group

Produced on paper from sustainable forests

This book is dedicated to the bereaved families
whose stories are told in this book,
to the many who offer support and care to them,
and to anyone who has suffered the pain of losing a child

Contents

Acknowledgements xii

Introduction 1
What type of care? 2
Religious, spiritual and pastoral care 3
Cultural care 6
For reflection 6

1 **Child palliative and bereavement care** 7
Issues in palliative and end-of-life care 7
Issues in bereavement and loss 15
Locating grief 16
Care pathways 18
Christianity and bereavement theory 19
For reflection 20

2 **Theological reflections on dying and death** 21
What are the questions from the families? 22
Reframing our dilemma 23
The 'God and suffering' debate 25
Some biblical reflections 28
Healing and miracles 35
Conclusion 38
For reflection 40

3 **Preparing to care** 41
What are we seeking to achieve? 42
Preparing to care: for everyone's SAKE 43
The roles we can play 51
Temptations in caring 53
Caring for carers and self-care 56
Connecting our theology and our pastoral care 60
For reflection 61

4 **Palliative care in practice** 62
Breaking bad news 63
Children's understanding of death 64
Relating to the dying child 68

	Planning for the death of a child	70
	Praying for help and healing	72
	For reflection	74
5	**Bereavement care in practice**	**75**
	Relating to bereaved families	75
	Insights from parents on what helps	78
	Insights from parents on what does not help	80
	Birthdays, Christmas and anniversaries	80
	Supporting siblings	82
	Grandparents – double grief	84
	Separated parents	86
	Fundraising and campaigning	86
	A new normal	88
	Conclusion	88
	For reflection	89
6	**Palliative care and bereavement in a hospital**	**90**
	Perspectives from medical staff	90
	Perspectives from non-medical staff	95
	Conclusion	99
	For reflection	99
7	**Palliative care and bereavement in the community**	**101**
	Organizations	111
	Conclusion	114
	For reflection	114
8	**Ethical issues**	**115**
	A brief introduction to ethics	115
	Factors and dynamics in families' ethical decision-making	117
	Ministerial ethics	119
	Medical ethics	119
	What might Christians add in making ethical decisions?	122
	A way forward	123
	For reflection	124
9	**Services, rituals and blessings**	**125**
	Why children's funerals and memorials are difficult	125
	Theological rationale for liturgical activities	126
	Principles for developing and delivering services	129
	Designing the service	134
	Leading services	138

Issues in rituals	142
End-of-life baptisms	143
Non-religious rituals and resources	145
Memorial services	146
Be mindful of how others interpret things	147
Some general tips	148
For reflection	148
Conclusion	**149**
Charter for palliative and bereavement care	149
Best practice	150
Top tips from families	151
Appendices	
1 Useful contacts and resources	153
2 Care pathways	157
3 Multi-faith perspectives	158
4 End-of-life baptism or blessing	162
5 Sample memorial service outline	165
6 Sources for liturgical material	166
7 Adult 'attitude to grief' scale	168
Bibliography	169
Index of biblical references	173
Index of names and subjects	174

Acknowledgements

My first thanks must go to all the children and families whose journeys I have been privileged to share. Their stories, whether told here or not, are the foundation of this book. And to those who are quoted here, I am extremely grateful for their willing help, openness and courage in allowing me to pass on their experiences and insights.

I also want to thank the many people who helped me with this book. I am grateful to the BCH Chaplaincy team and other staff at BCH who have been so generous in giving their time to write of their own experiences. Also those from the Paediatric Chaplaincy Network who came to a consultation day for the book, and to others who have contributed to the book from my wider network. Finally, thanks as always to my wonderful wife Sally, who contributed so much in making my hope of this book a reality.

The publisher and author acknowledge with thanks permission to reproduce extracts from the following:

Figures 1.1 and 1.2 are reproduced by permission of Richard Wilson.

'Some people come into our lives and quickly go' by Flavia Weedn © Archivea, <www.flaviaco.com>, reproduced by permission.

'Do not hurry as you walk with grief' from *Celtic Daily Prayers: Prayers and readings from the Northumbria community*. Reprinted by permission of HarperCollins Publishers Ltd © 2002 The Northumbria Community.

'Celebrating brief lives' is reproduced by permission of the Revd Pamela Turner.

'In the rising' by Rabbi Sylvan Kamens and Rabbi Jack Reimer from *Gates of Prayer: The New Union Prayerbook*, © 1975; under the copyright protection of the Central Conference of American Rabbis and reprinted for use by permission of the CCAR. All rights reserved.

Extracts from *Common Worship* are copyright © The Archbishops' Council, 2000, and are reproduced by permission.

Extract from *A New Zealand Prayer Book/He Karakia Mihinare o Aotearoa*, © 1997. Used with permission.

'Five candles': permission sought from S. L. Williams and D. Sims.

'Our pain in letting go': permission sought from SPCK.

Every effort has been made to seek permission to use copyright material reproduced in this book. The publisher apologizes for those cases where permission might not have been sought and, if notified, will formally seek permission at the earliest opportunity.

Introduction

> There's an elephant in the room.
> It is large and squatting, so it is hard to get around it.
> Yet we squeeze by it with 'How are you?' and 'I'm fine'...
> And a thousand other forms of trivial chatter.
> We talk about the weather.
> We talk about work.
> We talk about everything else ... except the elephant in the room.
> We all know it is there.
> We are thinking about the elephant as we talk together.
> It is constantly on our minds.
> For you see, it is a very big elephant.
> It has hurt us all.
> But we do not talk about the elephant in the room.
> Oh, please say the name.
> Oh, please say it again.
> Oh, please, let's talk about the elephant in the room.
> For if we talk about 'her' death,
> Perhaps we can talk about 'her' life.
> Can I say her name to you and not have you look away?
> For if I cannot, then you are leaving me
> Alone ... In a room ...
> With an elephant. (Author unknown)

> There are names for most forms of bereavement ... loss of a parent leaves you as an orphan. The loss of a partner leaves you a widow but the loss of a child ... there is no name and no one knows how to handle you.
> (Helen Philips)

The passion for this book arises from a desire to help and resource ministers, lay workers, youth, children and family workers, and all who come into contact with families who have lost or who are losing a child. While some of the material will be applicable for those with ministerial or other related training, I hope the book is relevant for those who may not have much experience but who want to learn to care better in this context.

The book reflects many journeys: mine as a senior chaplain at Birmingham Children's Hospital (BCH), and those of many patients, families, other professionals and colleagues I have worked with at BCH, both in the local community and from other hospitals. I write from the perspective of hospital visiting, but I hope that the lessons and principles I have learnt will be transferable to home visiting.

I hope the many stories and reflections in the book speak for themselves. They have been written, read and compiled with tears. Most of them are not anonymous, although this choice was offered, and every family wanted to use the real name of their child. The term 'child' is used generically to include babies, children and adolescents, unless it is an issue about a specific age group, and 'minister' is used inclusively of all those who care.

What type of care?

Some people have a tendency to use the terms 'spiritual' and 'religious' interchangeably but they can have different meanings. 'Religion' may be defined as a specific set of beliefs and practices, usually associated with an organized faith tradition such as Christianity, Islam or Judaism. 'Spirituality' may be defined as an individual's sense of peace, purpose, values, connection to others and beliefs about the meaning of life. Spirituality may be found and expressed through an organized religion or in other ways.

Many people consider themselves both spiritual and religious. Some may consider themselves spiritual, but not religious. Others may consider themselves religious, but not spiritual. When you add the term 'pastoral' to the mix it is clear that there are a range of different approaches to care in our context.

What is spirituality?

Narayanasamy (2001) identifies elements of spirituality in a healthcare context:

- the process of a sacred journey;
- the essence or life principle of a person;
- the experience of the radical truth of things;
- a belief that relates a person to the world;
- giving meaning and purpose in life;
- a life relationship or a sense of connection with mystery, higher power, God or universe.

This list gives a glimpse of the diversity of definitions that exist, the perspectives that nurses and other healthcare professionals may have and the somewhat woolly nature of the term! My working definition of spirituality is 'a lifelong journey on which people explore their connectedness to the world, themselves, others and possibly the transcendent, and the meaning and purpose of their lives; that which gives my life meaning and value'.

Religious, spiritual and pastoral care

There are many and various religious, spiritual and pastoral needs involved in supporting families in palliative and bereavement care. This support may be required at any time in the process. However, there is not a formula that we can use as needs vary between individuals and families, even if they notionally come from the same faith background. An essential task is thus to assess the needs and identify appropriate responses. Issues to explore include:

- religious faith (if any);
- religious and spiritual beliefs, particularly about death and the afterlife;
- practices or rituals that they use or would like to access;
- religious or spiritual concerns about treatment;
- connections to faith communities;
- religious and spiritual activities or resources that may be helpful;
- family relationships;
- others who may need support.

The responses to these and other issues may result in acts of religious, spiritual or pastoral care. This is what I mean by these terms:

- *Religious care* is care offered relating specifically to the tenets, practices, rituals and conventions of a particular religious faith.
- *Spiritual care* concerns itself with the big questions of life involving who someone is, and that person's purpose, destiny, identity and potential for a relationship with the transcendent.
- *Pastoral care* is a term used beyond a Christian context, for example in schools, and refers to care given to address the cares, concerns, problems, needs and issues of an individual or family.

If we were to draw these three areas as overlapping circles then it would be clear that some needs and responses fit all three definitions, some two, and some are discrete and clearly belong in one area or another.

George's story

To illustrate the differences between religious, spiritual and pastoral care I want to tell the story of one young person I had the privilege of knowing. George had leukaemia, and when I first knew him he had had a bone marrow transplant and was having fortnightly treatments at BCH. One of the side effects he faced was very fragile skin. This was not helpful as he was interested in and good at cooking. George had been referred by one of the psychologists supporting the family, who knew I used to be a chef and thought it might be good for George to talk to someone who could encourage and share his interests. I spent some time talking with George about cooking and seemed to gain some credibility for my four years as a chef at the Savoy and the Dorchester in London. Because of the condition of George's hands it was unlikely that he would be able to work in such an environment.

Pastoral care

This initial engagement was, I think, pastoral care. I was spending time with George, helping to while away an hour or so of his day visit to the hospital. The initial referral was thanks to my background as a chef, not my current vocation as a chaplain. I sought to communicate that I was interested in him, that I was concerned for his well-being and that I cared. He cooked with his mum at home, who assured me he was very good. We would chat about what he had been cooking at home, the type of things I used to enjoy cooking, and so on. I gave him a few mementos from my chef days, and he would bring me in samples of his cooking – it's a tough life having to eat cakes in the name of work! It is the crux of pastoral care to be present, spend time with people, listen intently, respond appropriately and meet the other's needs.

Spiritual care

Unbeknown to George, I thought it might be a rewarding experience for him to visit the kitchens of our hospital. On reflection, I think I not only wanted to do something nice for George but was also inspired by the example of organizations that are set up to help dreams come true for people with life-limiting illnesses. I discussed the possibility of George's visit with the catering manager, Tony. He was very accommodating and said he would do all he could to make this happen. I mentioned it to George's family and then to George, and he was so excited! So the momentous day came – but George was ill. We rearranged it and some of his family joined us.

Tony and the team were great with George. Tony introduced himself and explained that they did not do free tours of the kitchen: George would have to do some cooking first, with two of the senior chefs. George's eyes lit up and his whole body seemed to lift. But there was a problem, said Tony: George was not suitably dressed. At this point he brought out a jacket with George's name embroidered on it!

This, I think, was spiritual care. I was seeking to bring a sense of meaning to George's life, to give him a 'wow'-type moment and for him to experience something he could do that was fun and fulfilling. I sought to bring appropriate hope to George that he could have a future and should not give up, and to engage with his interests, values and questions concerned with his own individual, unique life and journey.

Religious care

Some time after this, George's condition became worse. When it became clear that there was no more that could be done for him, an end-of-life plan was made. George was going home in two days' time, to die. Completely out of the blue – well, at least to me – George asked me if I would baptize him. So we made arrangements to baptize him the next day in our hospital chapel. The wider family were invited and godparents arranged (further reflections on end-of-life baptisms are in Chapters 4 and 9). This was religious care, offering George a sign and sacrament of being welcomed into and belonging to God's family. George took his exploration in life to focus on the transcendent, other relationship with God, and expressed this in an end-of-life religious ritual that helped him and his family bring some closure and completion to his precious life.

I visited George at home the day before he died. There he was, in his bed with his Manchester United duvet cover; along with cooking we had conversations about football, and he got to me so much that I agreed to support Manchester United for Lent – not easy for a Chelsea supporter!

The family invited me to join the local vicar in taking George's funeral, which I gladly did. It was an awesome experience as his dad, a fireman, arranged a guard of honour for his son.

Now I am not saying it is always as neat and tidy as this. There is a great deal of overlap – for instance, George's spiritual needs were met through religious and pastoral care – and the spectrum of our care can be initiated at various points of need. Hopefully this gives an idea of how somewhat nebulous concepts can be worked out in practice.

George's life and death affected more than the usual ward and health-care staff: those from whom I had asked help – the kitchen staff, the person who made the badges and so on – had also been impacted by a life cut tragically short. It was a privilege knowing George, and I have been changed by the experience. I am not sure I was fully conscious that my engagement with George was so categorized. I sought just to come alongside him and his family and support them. This is my reflection after the event, and this story may give an indication of the spectrum of care our children's hospital chaplaincy team engage in. For all of us, we never know what direction our initial contact with a family will take us.

Cultural care

A final dimension of care is cultural care, which may or may not be related to religious and spiritual beliefs. Cultural issues affecting pastoral care may concern factors such as:

- who makes the decisions in the family;
- practices and rituals relating to death and bereavement – at one extreme, I supported a family who did not want to attend their child's funeral as the norm of their home country was that the wider community took care of this;
- choice of songs for a funeral;
- colour of clothing at funerals;
- preferences as to what the child or young person is told (or not told);
- burial or cremation.

For reflection

- What is your definition of spirituality?
- How do the concepts of religious, spiritual, pastoral and cultural care give an insight into different elements of your role?
- Have you experienced clashes in culture when seeking to offer care?

1

Child palliative and bereavement care

Cameron was a very happy, loving and sociable child with many friends; he was always smiling. Cameron was diagnosed with a malignant brain tumour in January 2005 at five years old. He had surgery, then high-dose chemotherapy for several months. He was classed as being in remission by October 2005, but by February 2006 the tumour had returned and he had two further operations to remove two tumours that were found. He then caught meningitis, which made him very ill and delayed the radiotherapy that he needed. He eventually recovered from the meningitis and started a six-week course of radiotherapy in May 2006. In September 2006 we found out that the tumour had returned again, and this time there was nothing further that the doctors could do. Cameron passed away in hospital on 29 October 2006 with his family by his side. Although Cameron had so many awful treatments he also had a lot of laughs in hospital and made friends there too. He was extremely brave and we are so very proud of him.

He looked up into the open rafters. 'I'm done, God,' he whispered. 'I can't do this any more. I'm tired of trying to find you in all of this.' And with that, he walked out the door. Mack determined that this was the last time he would go looking for God. If God wanted him, God would have to come find him.

(*The Shack*, Young, 2007, p. 80, a novel about a man whose child dies)

At Birmingham Children's Hospital there are around 200 deaths each year: 120 of them in the hospital, 80 in the community. In England and Wales in 2008 there were 3,369 deaths of children under one, 554 deaths of children aged one to four, 317 aged five to nine, 330 aged 10 to 14, 1,130 aged 15 to 19.

In this chapter we will establish a foundation and framework for the rest of the book, and give an overview of some of the key issues in paediatric palliative and bereavement care. Subsequent chapters will pick up and explore these issues in greater detail to enable us to be informed, effective and compassionate carers.

Issues in palliative and end-of-life care

Palliative care and end-of-life care can impact so many elements of a family's life, including physical, emotional, mental and cognitive, financial,

Key terms

- *Palliative care* The treatment of those who are going to die shortly – this might be days, weeks or months.
- *End-of-life care* The last 24–48 hours before a person dies.
- *Bereavement care* What is offered to a family after the death of their child. There is no time limit, although most care would be offered in the first year and for as long as a family perceived a need. Because of the nature of the bereavement journey, some don't access care until years later.
- *Life-limiting diseases* When certain conditions are diagnosed, e.g. cystic fibrosis, the family will know that it is likely their child will die prematurely. Such diseases have different life spans and children may move into palliative care as it becomes clear their life is nearing the end. 'Life-threatening illness of any sort presents existential challenges of isolation, meaninglessness, choice, and, of course, death itself' (Davy and Ellis, 2000, p. 15).
- *Terminal illness* A condition for which there is no known cure or for which no further effective treatment is available.

Relating to babies, these are the usual definitions used (from Cobb, 2005, p. 56):

- *Miscarriage or early pregnancy loss* The death of a baby before 24 weeks' completed gestation.
- *Stillbirth* The death of a baby after 24 or more weeks' completed gestation.
- *Perinatal death* The death of a baby who is stillborn or dies within the first seven days of life.
- *Neonatal death* Death in the first four weeks of life.

relational, behavioural and psychological. Which elements are impacted and to what extent may also be dependent on a range of family-specific factors, such as:

- the circumstances of the death
- the nature of relationships between the child and family
- religious beliefs
- ethnic and cultural norms
- the support structures available
- other responsibilities
- financial capacity, level of understanding of employer
- social skills, coping mechanisms
- personal well-being
- past experience
- closeness of home and hospital or hospice.

Upon diagnosis, or at least at the stage of palliative and end-of-life care, a range of issues need to be thought through and where possible agreed between family members, including:

- telling others – this is something that parents may appreciate help with; in a church context they may appreciate the congregation being told;
- telling children that they are dying – advice on how and when to do this will be given by the staff involved in the child's care;
- the wishes of the child;
- communication and relationships between close family and friends;
- keeping in touch with wider family and friends.

Once a diagnosis has been received parents may want to research the illness. The hospital will encourage them to find out as much as they can about it – the internet is a helpful resource – and to be involved in their child's treatment. This may throw up some possibilities. The first may be to get a second opinion on the diagnosis, which may be possible through the GP or may necessitate going privately, something outside the resources of many families. Another possibility is to be involved in clinical trials. This will need to be discussed with those in charge of the child's care and the benefits and drawbacks fully understood, if indeed it is possible at all.

There was an unspoken assumption that Chloe's family knew her condition was life limiting and therefore that they should not be surprised that she was dying, as they had had years to prepare. But that is not how it was. Living each day for today and packing life in was the approach. We didn't know when she was going to die. It was still a huge shock. We had seven years. (Chloe's mum)

Jan Burn (2005) has written about her experience of parenting a child with a life-threatening illness and suggests that people in her situation need to:

- learn to live with loneliness;
- learn to be flexible;
- discover the power of forgiveness;
- find freedom from guilt;
- prevent sibling rivalry;
- accept the necessity of rest;
- set boundaries.

These are common observations by parents and are helpful for us to remember when we are supporting families in this situation.

Responses to a diagnosis of terminal illness

It is important to remember that feelings of grief and loss belong to those who are receiving palliative care as well as to their families and friends – both before and after the child has died. Woodward uses the phrase 'living while dying' (2005, p. 29), which is an apt way of describing what children and families do when they become aware that there is no further life-saving care that can be given. In some ways they must get on with their lives, all the while knowing that they, or their child, or their brother or sister, may not see out the month. Lots of things can go on hold; lots of things can go into overdrive.

Responses to a diagnosis of terminal illness may include:

- *Disillusionment* Parents' hopes for their child's future are shattered.
- *Aloneness* Bonding and relationships may be more difficult for parents to establish with their child.
- *Inequality* Parents' perception of the unjustness and unfairness of what has happened may lead to a feeling of inequality in relation to other families.
- *Insignificance* Having a life-limited child may shatter parents' perceptions of rewarding parenthood.
- *Past orientation* Because the future may be uncertain, parents may focus on the past and look back on the time before diagnosis as one that was more secure. (Brown with Warr, 2007, p. 129)

One family I supported felt multiple loss when told their child only had a short time to live. All voiced the loss of the baby's future and their hopes, dreams and aspirations for him. Looking at each of these elements it is clear that there could be a wide range of conflicting emotions and perhaps uncharacteristic behaviour, with the potential of reacting badly to those who are trying to care if, for example, they have children who are not sick or who have achieved all the parents had hoped for their own children. We should also be aware that there can be hidden loss and grief through childlessness, abortion and IVF not working, for example. There are also issues for parents of children born with disabilities or life-limiting illnesses. Rachel Hill Brown reflects on her response to hearing her daughter had Down's Syndrome:

After ten attempts at IVF and a miscarriage we had given up on becoming parents of our own biological children. Years of heartache, broken dreams, repeated cycles of hope and loss had taken their toll on us in many ways. We had reached a point where we put in place defence mechanisms to survive the emotional trauma of being childless. The joy of her arrival was tempered by the questions and potential difficulties. Without doubt a gift and an arrival to celebrate, but with unanticipated ongoing grief and pain for the loss of the 'perfect' child we had anticipated. Learning to cope with the comments and questions of others has been one of the hardest areas to manage. The desire to protect her and to ensure that she gets all she needs in terms of support works in a creative tension with engaging as fully as possible with the world around us. The 'Why?' question is a natural one to ask. The answer is one that we will never know, and if we did it would make no difference to the situation. Each day our daughter teaches us more and more about what it is to be a human being.

The role of the parents

It is universally encouraged that parents be involved in the care of their child whatever the situation. Hospitals make it possible as far as they can for parents to stay with or near the child and there are often no formal visiting hours for families of children in hospital or hospice. The criteria will be:

- How much do the parents want to be involved?
- How much can they be involved?
- What training is needed and is the time frame feasible?

Parents should always raise such issues with staff treating their child, and if this is difficult then there are others such as chaplains or social workers who can help facilitate a conversation about how parents are involved.

Pressures on parents

It is helpful to be aware of the pressures that parents might feel. These may include:

- transport and travel time to and from hospital or hospice visiting, parking costs, the costs of eating out more through being away from home, etc.;
- employment, time off work, adjusting work hours;
- housing issues, such as alterations needed for equipment, access, etc.;
- finance, such as accessing benefit entitlement, possible funeral costs (most funeral directors do not charge for a basic funeral for a baby).

We may not always be able to offer direct support or advice in response to these pressures but the very least we can do is point families in the right direction.

One family I supported were so distressed by the news they were given that they not only went into shock but became overwhelmed by the choices they had to make. They became stuck and could not face any decisions. A member of the family observed what was happening and gave me permission to make some suggestions as to what we might do. This released them as they made short-term, small decisions on what to do next.

Hard letting anything else but grief into my head.

(Louisa's mum, Sharon Moore)

It is especially difficult for parents who want to be with their child when death comes but where it is not clear when this might happen. I have observed parents

- not wanting to leave;
- keeping vigil;
- ensuring that everyone has their contact numbers;
- feeling happier about leaving if someone else is staying with the child;
- wanting to honour the bravery of the child.

Families deal with these issues in a variety of ways, depending on the capacity of the parents and other family members to spend time with the child and their ability or otherwise to spend time in hospital and be around sick and dying children.

Helpful metaphors and images

Whirlpool

Figures 1.1 and 1.2 (overleaf) show one of the classic images used to describe what happens in grief, the image of a whirlpool devised by Richard Wilson (1993). They offer an image that goes far beyond the credit or power of mere words, illustrating the normality of life before the illness or death, the shock and awe of the waterfall, the turbulence of the whirlpool, and the power of the waterfall hitting the pool.

Rollercoaster

A rollercoaster ride is frequently used as an image for how it feels to have a child in palliative or end-of-life care. As a family member said to me, 'I want to get off but can't.' I suspect families arrive at this image when they stop and reflect on how they feel in the midst of all that is happening. As a carer, I sometimes reflect that, much as I may want to, I cannot join them on their ride. However, our journey with the family may feel as if we are on our own ride.

My son Mitchel was diagnosed during the early stages of a twin pregnancy with a severe heart defect. Prospects looked hopeful that surgery and ongoing treatment were possible, with a heart transplant likely in the future. However, full diagnosis would be at birth and unfortunately it was the worst outcome. The conflict and utter devastation of this news,

Figure 1.1 The river of life, the waterfall of loss, the whirlpool of grief, the cliffs of reality

alongside the absolute joy of seeing both my babies born after such an arduous pregnancy, was simply mind-blowing.

How can you possibly know how to express, as a young person (only 18), the quality and quantity of support and care that is needed at such a time? I can only say I felt physically and emotionally battered and ripped apart and seemed to exist in sort of a bubble. I ate little, slept little, sobbed a lot and felt thoroughly sick most of the time.

I had an emergency caesarean. Immediately my son was taken to special care and I cared for my daughter. My son was subsequently transferred to BCH and I was allowed home with only one baby. From this point on the invaluable work of many special people began. It was to become

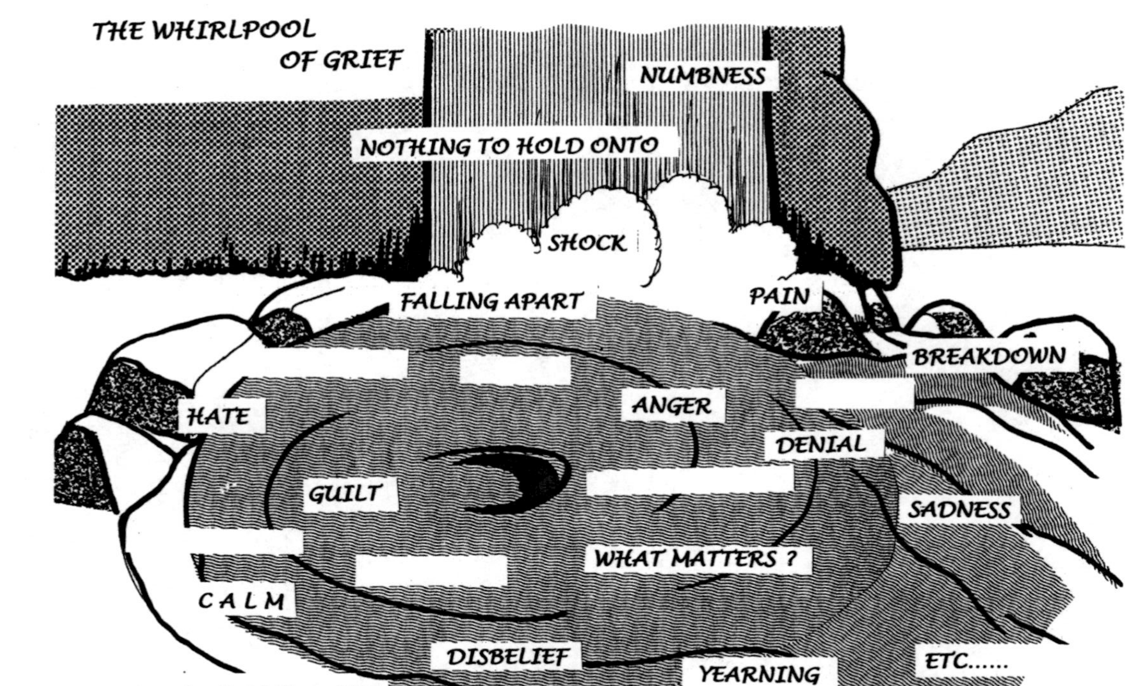

Figure 1.2 The whirlpool of grief

a rollercoaster of emotions and events I would never want to wish on anyone, but with a lot of support I am here to tell you more.

Other images that families have shared with me that might be helpful include:

- being lost in a maze;
- being on overload;
- having no petrol left in the tank;
- wearing a mask;
- feeling physically wounded or shot.

End-of-life care

It may be of great surprise that many deaths are not sudden or unexpected: they are planned. A consequence of this is that, with some families, there can be a discussion of where the child will die. This may include the following:

- Where does the family want the child to die?
- Where is it feasible for the child to die?
- What medical or community resources are needed?
- What illness does the child have?

Options of where to die would be hospital, hospice or home.

Children receiving treatment in hospital may die after withdrawal of treatment, and this will be planned and usually agreed with the family, giving them the option to bring in other family members, have a blessing or baptism or other ritual, and have the opportunity to say goodbye in the way they wish. This only happens when there are no other possibilities for treatment, when the appropriate tests have been done and when this is deemed to be in the best interests of the child. At other times children will die suddenly or semi-suddenly; at BCH, this is probably only about half of the deaths.

Issues in bereavement and loss

> If bereavement is a wound, then grief is the inflammation that follows. It causes pain, swelling and disturbance of function. It can last a long time and may leave scars. Yet it is the process by which healing occurs.
>
> (Wilson, cited in Lane Fox, 2005, p. 25)

It is a natural process, but one which can cause discomfort in others and confusion in ourselves. I often hear reports that people were so helpful up until the funeral but that beyond it much help and support just melted away. Grieving parents can feel as though they should have moved on and people may begin to avoid them, not knowing what to say or do. Equipping churches and others to care for those facing loss and bereavement is a significant and important ministry and fulfils the mandate of Isaiah 61.1 to bind up the broken-hearted. Lane Fox expresses some of the difficulties that parents face. This quotation raises so many of the pertinent issues that those caring for the bereaved encounter:

> These different ways of dealing with grief can put a significant strain on a parent's relationship. It is helpful for them to understand that their partner's response to grief is natural and to find ways of sharing their feelings and reach out to one another. Grieving is an essential and necessarily painful healing process. It means feeling and expressing all the emotions you have. It also means slowly accepting the reality of what has happened and learning to live with the change that has taken place in your life. Facing life without someone you love is difficult and painful. No one can fill the aching void, and each day can bring constant reminders of their absence. Just getting through the day can seem an insurmountable task. The future may seem uncertain or even frightening. One of the most difficult aspects of grieving is the feeling of being out of control. Grief is a solitary, messy, exhausting and relentless business, but it is survivable. As human beings, we have infinite resources within ourselves to heal and move forward, if only we first allow ourselves the time to express the pain.
>
> (Lane Fox, 2005, p. 27)

Locating grief

Grief can be located in wider loss theory: the more losses experienced, the greater the potential for complicated grief (see below). Losses in relation to bereavement include relational, role and systemic losses as the family changes, an individual's role within it changes and relationships both end and change.

The bereavement journey

There are a range of responses to bereavement and each person will have a unique journey. Common responses to grief include shock, disbelief, anger, blame, guilt, pain, struggling to cope, helplessness, horror, drawing on faith and loss of faith.

At the same time, the way in which people deal with grief may be affected by a range of factors, including age, gender, ethnicity, cultural norms, relationship to the child, mental capacity, previous experience of loss, and family roles and responsibilities.

Theories that delineate phases of grief are not necessarily to be seen as stage-by-stage processes that people move through; the journey is more complex than that and people may move in and out of different phases.

Table 1.1 seeks to parallel some of the theories of grief to each other.

Table 1.1 Theories of grief

Phase	*Engel (in Speck, 1978)*	*Kübler-Ross*	*Bowlby*
1	Denial	Denial	Numbness
2	Developing awareness	Rage and anger	Pining
		Bargaining	Disorganization
		Depression	
3	Resolution	Acceptance	Re-organization

One of the critiques of a linear process of grief is that it does not reflect grief's complexity. It has been observed that people may seem to go through the process stage by stage but may then be deemed to be grieving inappropriately when they revisit previous emotions or express new ones, or manifest negative characteristics such as withdrawal. The image of a spiral of grief is better, and if shared this encourages and if necessary gives permission and reassurance that revisiting shock, despair or denial is part of normal grieving.

Complicated grief

It could be said that all grief is complicated. Loss is difficult to handle, but theory suggests multiple loss is what can push us over the edge. The loss of a child may be the initial loss which we seem to cope with, but when we lose our car keys it sends us over the top. It is clear the issue is not the car keys but the cumulative loss, leading to unmanageable stress, that manifests itself in an over-reaction to a seemingly insignificant event. There are a variety of factors that affect complicated grief:

- accumulated loss
- liberating grief
- unexpected or sudden death
- parents or family at different points of letting go or coming to terms with loss
- unresolved loss
- guilt and/or shame
- other children involved
- genetic diagnosis.

This is a diverse list and much of child bereavement would involve one or several of these. We could conclude, then, that most child bereavements are likely to be complicated.

When to refer

This is difficult to state categorically, but the main criterion we use is similar to that in other areas of ministry: we should refer when the family member is at risk of causing harm to him- or herself or others. This raises the question: what is harm? It is difficult to define, as we all handle grief in different ways and at a different pace. If in doubt, if you are concerned that grief is being handled in an unhealthy manner, encourage the person to go to his or her general practitioner (GP) (see the GP's contribution to Chapter 7, p. 102).

Can death ever be welcomed?

This sounds like a very strange question. It is frequently easy to answer in relation to a 92-year-old in pain with multiple illnesses, but what about when it is a three-week-old baby? My experience of supporting many families is that it can happen. Death can be a liberating experience, even the death of a child. This may seem a harsh thing to say and we may be tempted to judge, but can we imagine what it must be like either to see your child suffer day after day, without hope of recovery, or to know your child is just going to get worse and never better? We need to stop and consider that a parent in this impossible position may simultaneously want the child to live and to die and so not suffer any more. How is this not the most natural parental feeling in the world? One of the saddest things I see in my work is when parents then beat themselves up for feeling this way.

There are a variety of factors that impact the extent to which bereavement is liberating:

- timing
- support structure
- long-term prognosis
- prejudice of family and community
- quality of life
- level of suffering
- capacity of parents
- community resources.

The important thing is to help those who are grieving to identify, own and process the myriad feelings that emerge at such a time.

Care pathways

Hospitals, hospices and community healthcare staff have processes to follow which are based on what is regarded as best practice for the patient. One of these processes is called a pathway. It is a list of steps that are followed, frequently by way of a flow chart, to ensure all the necessary issues and procedures take place. There are pathways for both palliative and bereavement care, and it can be useful to know that they exist and what is included in them. One of the important aspects of care pathways for ministers to be aware of is that religious, spiritual and/or cultural care will be found both in national guidelines for pathways and in most local examples in hospitals, hospices and community care; further information can be found in Appendix 2. It will be useful for the rest of the book for you to know the BCH Chaplaincy bereavement care pathway.

Stages in the Birmingham Children's Hospital bereavement care pathway

End-of-life rituals

Offer of blessings or baptisms (hospital, home or hospice).
Attend visits to hospital viewing suite.

Funerals

Available for funerals (prefer to take with local clergy).

Send

Religious or spiritual support booklet is sent about ten days after the death (according to religion or none).
Invitation to have an inscription in our book of remembrance.
Anniversary cards.

Offer

Ongoing support.
Booklets for siblings.

Invitations to events

Annual memorial service (Christian).
Annual walk and picnic at the National Memorial Arboretum.

Christianity and bereavement theory

Some of the key concepts in bereavement theory resonate with my Christian worldview – words such as 'grief', 'fear', 'acceptance'. My question is: do we give enough permission to grieving families to engage with feelings and emotions that might be seen as 'not very Christian', such as denial or anger? Another question is: how gracious and patient are we with those who irritate us when they seemingly never move on, or go back to the beginning more frequently than we find comfortable? We have the opportunity to engage with the transcendent in the midst of immanent feelings, without condemnation but with liberty.

The incomplete truth that time is a great healer must be engaged with. From the stories told both by our families and in literature, it is clear that this is only half the story: love is a greater healer than time. The love of family, friends, carers, ministers and the Christian community to know, feel and receive God's love for them in their situation is a much more effective healer. I will pick up the outward expressions of this in the rest of the book.

> Time does not heal
> It makes a half stitched scar
> That can be broken and you feel
> Grief as total as in its first hour.
> (Anon; from Lapwood, 1992, p. 24)

For reflection

- How have you identified loss outside physical bereavement?
- How have you dealt with your own loss and grief in the past? Did you get appropriate support?
- How have you responded to friends or colleagues who have lost a child?
- Where are the organizations or people that offer support to bereaved parents in your community?
- Are there strategies to consider implementing in your church to help support those who have lost children?

2

Theological reflections on dying and death

There is a Christian family which I [Kathryn Darby, BCH chaplain] have been visiting who describe their experience as a living hell. Their child was born with a rare and inoperable brain tumour. A course of chemotherapy was started. The tumour, untreated, will almost certainly lead to death; however, the prognosis with treatment is not hopeful. Martin, the father, told me of the benefits of sharing with other families facing similar difficulties. He told me, 'Meeting with other families on the ward has been good. I have been asking myself, "Why? Why me? Why us?" Recently, I met another family, and they were asking the same question: they were the mirror image of us. Hearing it from them, I realized that I had to stop, because there aren't any answers. I just have to accept that this is the situation and we have to move on from here. It's no use asking over and over, "Why?" We just have to try to go on from here.' Martin continued, 'I had been feeling frustrated with everything, and everyone in the hospital. I started to react to everything, and be critical of everything that was said. But then, I decided I have to stop that too, because everyone is doing all that they can to help Nathan. He has had eight operations, and they are trying everything. I had to change my perspective. But I feel like I am walking around with a cloud hanging over my head. Maybe this is happening because of all the bad things I have done in my life. God is trying to teach me a lesson.'

At this point in the conversation, I had to disagree, while acknowledging that I have heard others begin to wonder if God is punishing them through their suffering. 'What kind of a God,' I asked, 'would want to teach you a lesson through the suffering of your child? What sort of a God would that be? Not one that I want to worship. If it is the case, that God looks down on us and sends lightning bolts on some people to teach them a lesson or to punish them into obedience and good behaviour, then I am going to stop worshipping God today. I don't believe God is like that.' I think there is some inner liberation to be found in rising beyond the question 'Why did it happen?' to begin to ask the question 'What do I do now that it has happened?' (Kushner, 2000, p. 79).

Disease is part of the world we live in. The Christian message is that God does not abandon us in our suffering, but cares for us, and holds on to us, even through the darkest of times. If that is true, I suggested, speaking to Martin, then you are precious to God, God loves each of you, in

> the family, very much. Is it possible to hear the whisper from God, 'I love you. I understand the torment that you are going through, and I want to care for you'? Opportunities to articulate theology are more of a rarity than a common occurrence. People who are in the thick of a personal crisis rarely want to have a theological discussion, and often my mind would go blank if they did. For the most part, as people responding to the needs of others, chaplains have to carry within us the belief in a loving, caring God, and try, through our actions and listening, to imitate Christ, to offer a supportive presence, to witness to the love of God. Remaining familiar with the stories of the faith and reminding ourselves daily of God's steadfast love keeps us alive to a message of hope and saving grace for others, when the people we are visiting can no longer hope, and their hearts are heavy with a load of care and weariness.

This story introduces us to many of the faith and theological issues raised when we discuss our care of dying children. It has been suggested that if you can do theology at the bedside of a dying child you can do theology anywhere. In this chapter I seek to be honest about my own journey and those I have travelled with. My field is practical theology (not biblical studies or systematic theology) and this chapter indicates how I reflect on my practice and the experiences and reality of a dying child and my faith. In my ministerial experience I have encountered nothing more difficult than this.

I began my Christian journey in the evangelical stream of the Church. This chapter represents my personal struggle with the teaching I heard that 'nothing happens outside of God's will' in the light of what I see in the hospital. I am very aware of the tension between the faith I bring and apply to my work (applied theology) and the faith I seek to work out in the midst of a children's hospital (theological reflection). I have changed some of the things I believe in the light of seeking to apply and work them out in the light of my experiences. This is a scary yet exciting journey. I am comfortable with the idea that there are questions but find it hard when I hear answers that misrepresent what I understand about the Christian faith and God. Offering specific answers can sometimes be cold comfort – we feel better for being able to give an answer but it may be of little use.

What are the questions from the families?

There are many questions that have been asked in seeking to make sense of children dying, such as:

- Why does God allow suffering, permit my child to suffer?
- What have I done for this to happen, to deserve this? Whose fault is it?

- Why doesn't God do something?
- What happens to a child when he or she dies?
- Will I see my child again?

So what are our options in making faith sense of questions?

- God decides which children live and die.
- God created a world and humanity with choice and consequences.
- There are other factors at work, e.g. evil, Satan, according to our personal theology and faith tradition.

We also have some ministerial questions that arise out of these and other questions:

- What of God and the kingdom do we seek to imitate and implement in our care?
- What are we working towards achieving? Care, healing, miracles?
- What can we pray for?

My experience suggests that formulaic answers do not work but that we do need to be able to offer something in response to these questions.

Reframing our dilemma

An approach I find helpful is to look at reframing the issue. I do not wish to be trite with the complexity of our quandary, but many books have been written about suffering and I do not have either the skills or the space to reproduce the spectrum or difficulty of the debate. I would like to contribute to the debate by reframing it in this way:

The story is told of a minister whose wife died in a car crash, leaving a five-year-old daughter, shortly after he moved to a new church. What he said at the funeral was this:

> I don't know why God let my wife suffer so much pain and die like she did in that car crash . . . But I do know this, that Jesus died for us all and rose again. That Jesus has promised eternal life to all those who trust in him. And what I do know helps me to live with what I don't know.
> (Mitton and Parker, 1991, p. 28)

I find such thoughts help me engage equally seriously with both suffering and faith. It reminds me that I have a God who is love and who loves the dying child, the bereaved family. These are not contradictory facts but tensions on the journey. My reflection on my own losses adds to this: 'What I do have helps me with what I don't have.' Theology offers faith and beliefs that shape and inspire me, constrain and direct who I am and who I am to 'be' with these children and families.

Unhealthy equations

> 'Is there a God?' asked the Marxist.
> 'Certainly not the kind people are thinking of,' said the Master.
> 'Whom are you referring to when you speak of people?'
> 'Everyone.' (de Mello, 1985, p. 151)

I do not believe families have the wrong questions, but they do have the wrong equation. They take their understanding of the Christian faith, what they have heard in church, from family, the media, etc., and seek to make sense of the death of their child. Their equations go something like these:

- God made the world and is in control.
- Therefore, everything that happens in this world is what God plans, wills or desires.
- Therefore, my child dying is God's will, because God knows what he is doing and knows best.

Or

- My child is dying, has died. This is not good.
- Life goes on, and in due course good things come out of the death of my child: I grow; I appreciate things I would not otherwise appreciate; others are changed because of my child's life; I learn things I would not otherwise have learnt.
- Therefore, it must have been God's will, plan and divine purpose that my child has died.

Or

- Life is supposed to be fair.
- What is happening to my child is not fair.
- Therefore, God is not being fair with my family.
- God is not the friend of our family.

In response to such equations, every fibre of my body wants to shout, 'NO, that's not right!' They demonstrate how, if our original premises are incorrect, the answers we get will be flawed.

A healthy equation

I want to suggest that to understand the suffering of children we need to change the elements of the equation to embrace other things we know about God, including:

- God loves your child and your family.
- God is for you, not against you.
- God is with you and has not abandoned you.
- God created a world and humanity with choice and consequences.

- There are other factors at work.
- This illness is not a judgement from God.
- This illness is not a test from God.
- It is not just a matter of finding the right amount of faith or the right prayer – there are no formulae.
- God did not plan this. God is outside of our time frame and there is a difference between knowing and determining.
- Not everything that happens in our world and our lives is what God wants or desires.
- We have a redemptive faith that can bring good out of bad, negative, evil situations.
- In the end, when all is said and done, we do not really understand suffering.

I do not want to be superficial in the application of my equation; there may be exceptions to some of what I am proposing and there are other factors we must take into account. We do well to remember that:

- God cannot contradict his own nature, values or being;
- we have a mysterious God who is Spirit and works in mysterious ways and beyond our human understanding. God is God.

A parent said to me, 'I will never find a reason why Louisa died, but there is a reason why she was alive, but it is not yet all clear why.' I find this so helpful; it is real, redemptive and hopeful.

The 'God and suffering' debate

Sometimes I think I am beginning to gain an insight into this debate, yet a day later I can think I have no understanding whatsoever. I have concluded that I will never have a complete, thoroughly robust answer that will stand up to every scrutiny and challenge. A part of me is satisfied with this, but another part is immensely frustrated and annoyed that I don't have such an answer to this most commonly asked question. Issues usually raised in the traditional debate are:

- the free will of humanity
- the fall of humanity, the world, sin and its consequences
- evil, Satan, demons
- the natural order;

in relation to and tension with

- an all-powerful, all-loving, compassionate, merciful God
- a God who does not seem to intervene and stop suffering or children dying.

I believe we are called to live and minister in this tension. Hauerwas offers a partial insight into this dilemma, suggesting that

> Formulating the problem of suffering in its conventional statement revolves around the seeming contradiction between the divine power and the divine love. If God is loving and at the same time all-powerful, then why is there so much suffering in the world? The assumption is that the deity could, if the deity would, simply eliminate suffering.
>
> (cited in Barritt, 2005, pp. 57–8)

However, Hauerwas would not necessarily see this as a good thing. He argues,

> I have always thought it odd that anyone should think it possible or even a good thing to eliminate all suffering. Suffering, I have been taught, is not something you eliminate, but something with which you must learn to live . . . without allowing ourselves and others to suffer we could not be human or humane. For it is our capacity to feel grief and to identify with the misfortune of others which is the basis for our ability to recognise our fellow humanity. (cited in Barritt, 2005, p. 55)

Easier, perhaps, to accept from the position of a carer than the one being cared for in our context.

Another important aspect of this debate is what we understand as and call disasters, such as earthquakes, tsunamis, droughts, etc. Farley sees suffering through such events as an inevitable dimension of living within the type of creation that has been given to us. 'To have a world that was not fragile and did not contain the possibility of tragedy would be to have a different creation to the one in which we reside' (cited in Swinton, 2007, p. 62). Creation is flawed and sick, and dying children are a part of that.

Humanity is created with the capacity for free will and choice, and this is a wonderful gift and ability. It is a part of what it means to be made in the image of God and gives us the capacity to bless ourselves, each other and our world. But it also accounts for a great deal of the pain and suffering of children. Humanity has a great deal of choice when it comes to how we treat children and the attitudes we have to those who do not measure up to the current cultural conception of perfection.

Fiddes articulates what is perhaps the most common approach to theodicy – that of free will:

> God's purpose in creating the universe was to make a world of personal beings with whom God could enter into a relationship. For them to be real persons they must have been created free to do either good or evil; the only other option was a world of puppets and robots. If doing the right is to have any meaning there must be the alternative of doing the wrong (evil), with all the suffering this entails. (Fiddes, 2000, p. 164)

I believe in the reality of personal and corporate sin. Sometimes it is clear where responsibility lies; other times it is more difficult. When the media report that an adult has physically abused a child, it is the parent who has sinned against the child and the immediate and wider community, and it is the parent who is condemned. I want to suggest it is not always as simple as this. Yes, the adult is responsible without question, but what are the circumstances behind this? We often find that behind a great deal of suffering is a great deal of complexity.

We are confused when the abuser is a fellow child. We ask, 'How could this have happened?' When we see starving children we ask, 'Why?' We seem much more aware today of the correlation of poverty and suffering to the responsibility and response of the international community and its policies. However, we have become so confused that when we see reports of child neglect not being picked up by social services we blame lack of diligence in local government. I think we confuse responsibility: the adult is responsible for harming the child; local provision can only be responsible for not picking up signs of it happening and potentially preventing it happening. Social services are not responsible for the neglect: the parent is. The significant question becomes, 'But to what degree?' I will return to the issue of pastoral response to this in Chapter 3.

There is such a spectrum of what we understand by evil, but we must at least acknowledge the potential of evil in a conceptual or personalized sense to affect the well-being of humanity. Swinton proposes two theological perspectives of evil: first, moral – human failure or actions, individual and corporate – and second, natural occurrences – earthquakes, diseases, etc., over which we have no control (Swinton, 2007, pp. 50–1). Whatever our theology, we are unwise to absolutely rule out the influence of supernatural or human expression of evil in children's illnesses. Why is it important to take evil seriously? 'Evil is that which destroys hope in the love of God' (Swinton, 2007, p. 59).

As one of my earlier equations suggests, one starting point for some families is 'It's not fair.' This is so understandable, but it starts from another wrong premise: that life is supposed to be fair. My response is, 'Who says?' Almost every news bulletin confirms that it isn't. I did an end-of-life blessing for a teenager whose life-limiting disease had just been rediagnosed as terminal. The father got very angry after the short ceremony and started to kick the wall. I never know what to expect a family member to do or say at such a time. He approached me outside the cubicle and said, 'It's just s★★★★y,' several times. He was understandably upset with the sadness of it all, but at that moment, when he might justifiably have asked 'Why?' he just stated it was 's★★★★y'. My response was to agree with him: 'Yes, it is.'

Because I don't expect life to be fair I don't make this type of statement or question and therefore I do not blame God when things go wrong in my life. When we were not able to conceive children, it would have been very easy for us to blame God. We had questions; we were confused and hurt and wondered where God was. We had to make sense of our circumstances in the light of the God whom we knew to be faithful. Our reflections led us to conclude that our bodies were imperfect through being a part of an imperfect world – all human beings have something wrong with them and this was the way it manifested in us. Some might see this as a divine conspiracy, but we drew upon what we did know about God and can honestly say that we feel fulfilled and blessed in what he has given us rather than frustrated in what we do not have. It seems reasonable and more than understandable that families cry for justice; to see a child dying is not just, it's not fair. We must not confuse the facts that our God is just but our world is not, and it is a wrong element of the equation that because God is just when our world isn't, it is because God isn't being fair.

Another theological rationale we hear used is God's providence, the belief that God plans everything, that God preordains the course that our lives will take. The Jewish nation of the Old Testament believed in just such a God. If something good happened it was because God did it, and subsequently if something bad happened it was ordained by God. One of the observations I have of how Christians seek to make sense of events in our lives and in our world is that we give God either credit or blame. We sometimes seem to be only able to make sense of the situation if we perceive God to be the initiator. My reflection is that we are in danger of giving God the blame or credit where it is not due. I am not seeking to undermine the power and omnipotent nature of our God, but to ask, 'Are there any other possibilities as to why this child is dying?' I am not sure I could support so many dying children and their families if I believed their illness was the will and plan of God. As chaplains, we spend a lot of time explaining the sort of God we don't believe in.

Some biblical reflections

Have you ever noticed the Bible stories about dying and dead children? There are stories of children being sick and dying (2 Samuel 12.1–31, David and Bathsheba's child; 1 Kings 17.1–24, Elijah and the widow's son; 2 Kings 4.1–44, Elisha and the Shunammite's son). There are recordings of mass murder or genocide (Exodus 1.15–22, Pharaoh and the killing of the firstborn males; Matthew 2.16–18, Herod and the killing of the innocents). We also have the story of the plague on the firstborn (Exodus

12.29). Several of these texts seem to suggest God's involvement, if not instigation. When we read these passages and try to identify why the children died it seems to be God's judgement, to show God's glory and as a consequence of sin. It is no wonder, when Christians seek to make sense of these Scriptures, that they can end up with a God who has decided in advance what will happen to us. However, a question we need to ask is whether this is the God of the whole Bible, of our Christian faith and tradition. The answer is clearly no. We are in danger of taking a particular instance and universalizing it and saying that God kills children.

'The Lord struck the child'

Take, for example, the story we find in 2 Samuel 12, where we see King David as a parent responding to the death of the child that has just been born to him by Bathsheba. Before the child died he acted in such a way as to try and get God to be gracious, but once the child died it seemed to be life as usual again: now he is dead there is no need to grieve. This manifestation is often seen in families whose children have long-term illnesses, then die. It is as though they have done their grieving while the child is alive.

But I think David is showing us more than this. He is revealing his understanding of God. He thinks by his repentance he can persuade God to let his child live, that God is in control of the life and death of his child. After the child dies, David gets back on with his life and there is no further recording of his grief. The question I have from the earlier part of the story is about the child dying either as a substitute for David's sin or as punishment. Nathan says to David, 'Now the LORD has put away your sin; you shall not die. Nevertheless, because by this deed you have utterly scorned the LORD, the child that is born to you shall die' (2 Samuel 12.13–14). Is the author writing here out of direct revelation or seeking to make sense of what has happened? The writer goes on to say: 'Then Nathan went to his house. The LORD struck the child that Uriah's wife bore to David, and it became very ill' (v. 15). It is also interesting to note that the child is given no name. I want to ask whether there are other ways to understand the interaction between God and humanity than one involving the idea of a God who preordains the death of a child. This is one of the unhelpful beliefs our families have through taking a particular situation and applying it to themselves. It is impossible to know about the condition of the child, or whether David continued to grieve, or about the grief of the child's mother, Bathsheba. We can conclude that David was manifesting cultural and religious grief and that this story is not designed to give us a model for expressing our grief or for understanding our God today.

'The hand of God has struck me'

Job is one of the most interesting and challenging books when it comes to understanding suffering and death. Among all his losses are his ten children in something like a tornado. Job's response to his endless tragedies is to say, 'the LORD gave, and the LORD has taken away; blessed be the name of the LORD' (1.21). The next verse says that 'In all this, Job did not sin by charging God with wrongdoing'. But Job changes his mind, and begins to blame God: 'have pity on me, have pity on me, O you my friends, for the hand of God has touched me!' (19.21). Job's friends certainly hold to a theology of bad things happening when you sin and don't confess it. They think God has done these things directly to Job and therefore he must have sinned, so he should confess his sin and maybe God will bless him again. No wonder Job is confused: his worldview is that God blesses when you are good and curses when you are bad, but he has not been bad. Job desires justice, and he concludes that this is not fair. It is understandable that, even today, people move to this position. Humans have a tendency to want to blame someone or something for what goes wrong.

> When my child was dying of cancer ten years ago, fellow Christians asked me if I had any unconfessed sin in my life. They questioned if I had enough faith. They only added to my pain and isolation. I realize today that these believers were scared. They wanted to find something wrong with me to assure them that they would never face this tragedy. Most people still don't understand. God did heal my child, just not on this side of heaven where I can see it yet. (cited in Froehlich, 2000, p. 48)

This story, told by Kathryn Darby, one of the BCH Chaplaincy team, highlights that one of the first questions we must ask ourselves is 'What is God like?' What is the nature and character of God? If we do not initially internally answer this question then we are in danger of being externally pastorally inappropriate. The trouble with the death of a child is that it seems to turn upside down, inside out, all we thought and knew about God. That God is love is core to the Christian faith, as is the idea that God is merciful. When we don't see God as loving or merciful this can cause us problems: our faith is shaken.

Children may blame themselves for their suffering

Tom wondered if he was somehow to blame for his brain tumour and deserving of his suffering. As I sat down in the chair alongside the bed, his first words to me were, 'I'm scared.' At that moment the nurse entered the room to adjust his lines and treatment. Not unusually, in the hospital setting conversations and prayers may be interrupted, and the lack of privacy at times is particularly difficult for adolescents, who are often acutely self-conscious. I was aware, too, that Tom's mother, who was sitting within earshot, had asked the nursing staff to be economical with the truth about Tom's prognosis.

After some exchanges about home and school, Tom's mum gently asked him if there was something he wanted to 'ask about God'. He nodded and launched in, explaining his fear that he had done something to bring this suffering upon himself, that he might be to blame. I stated clearly that I did not believe in a God who made children suffer. Nor did I remotely believe that Tom had in any way brought this situation upon himself. God did not wake up on Monday and decide who was going to be sent to hospital that day. God loved every child, and certainly loved Tom as much as any other child.

'Then why did he do this? Why didn't he stop me from getting sick?' The questions were fired back at me.

I acknowledged to myself again and to him how difficult and unanswerable this question is. There are no easy answers, as I said to Tom. I went on to say, 'We live in a world in which innocent people suffer, and there is no obvious reason why some people become ill and other people don't. But it is not your fault. It's just the way things are. One thing we can hold on to is that we live in an age when there are good medicines, and you are in an excellent hospital and will receive the best treatments for getting better.' It was important to me to categorically reject the idea that Tom was to blame, or any notion of a punitive God, while also trying to engender hope.

'A time to die'

Another verse reflecting the Old Testament's understanding of death and dying is found in Ecclesiastes 3.2–3: 'a time to be born, and a time to die; a time to plant, and a time to pluck up what is planted; a time to kill, and a time to heal'. This is reflected in what I hear from families: 'Well, it was just his time', 'God has called her home.' Ecclesiastes 3.1–8 is in a different writing style from that which comes before and after it, and should probably be best understood as something like a poem. It has rhythm, scans and could even be an existing piece of writing inserted into the text. We could understand these verses to mean that God decides when children or people are to be born and to die, to be killed or to be healed; or it may be that the author is writing about an understanding of the cycle of life which includes death, not saying that God has preordained it. Unfortunately it is all too simple to read such verses and conclude that hit and run, cancer, suicide, was God's will for this child. That is somewhere I choose not to go and one reason why

I don't read this passage at any funerals, let alone a child's – I don't want to risk the misinterpretation and consequential misperception of the nature of God.

'Fearfully and wonderfully made'

Psalm 139 is so often quoted in support of God's knowledge and care for us as individuals. However, there are some very interesting challenges arising from reflection upon the suffering of children in relation to this psalm. How can we make sense of children who are born with disabilities in the light of verses 13 and 14a: 'For it was you who formed my inward parts; you knit me together in my mother's womb. I praise you, for I am fearfully and wonderfully made'? David could be reflecting on his own physical body, which we know is good-looking (1 Samuel 17.42), and thinking about how uniquely human beings are made by God. When we take these verses in context they help us to understand how we can say this of children who are miscarried, stillborn, detected with illnesses on scans or born with illnesses. The phrase 'inward parts' here is from a word that translated from the Hebrew literally means 'kidneys', but in relation to Jewish thought at the time means 'spirit', the essence of who we are (Van Gemeren in Longman and Garland, 2008, p. 838). Psalm 139.16 says that 'Your eyes beheld my unformed substance. In your book were written all the days that were formed for me, when none of them as yet existed.' A literal interpretation of this verse could suggest that God has preordained the years and days of our lives, suggesting that if a child dies this was God's plan for him or her. I find it more helpful to see God as outside of time and foreknowing, not preordaining.

'Consider it nothing but joy'

There are various passages that suggest we should praise God and rejoice in respect of trials that we face, with James 1.2–4 being perhaps the most well known and the hardest to make sense of in our context. There are verses in the epistles which I think have been misunderstood. When we look at verses such as Romans 5.3, James 1.2 and 1 Peter 1.6, which speak of the benefits of suffering, the context of this suffering is not general but persecution. Because this has not been explained in our teaching, some Christians and ministers have then misunderstood this type of verse and have assumed that when they face horrible situations such as their child dying they should rejoice, because God has seen them as worthy of handling such testing. I cannot tell you how angry this type of exegesis and application makes me. I am not suggesting that the writers were only referring to rejoicing when you are persecuted for being a Christian, but when we misapply them to mean we should be thankful to God when children are sick and dying I think we present a distorted view of who God is and what he wants from us.

Scholars may be able to give erudite explanations of these passages, but someone picking up a Gideon Bible at the bedside of a sick child doesn't have the benefit of an understanding of genres of writing, the cultural context of the passages and so on. A 14-year-old girl wrote this, and I sympathize with the sentiments:

> Why does God not listen? The Bible tells us 'Ask and you will receive.' Why did God take Violet? I JUST DON'T UNDERSTAND! I'm so frustrated! Sometimes I just want to curl up in a ball and SCREAM! I don't want to say this but I am very angry with God. I get upset when people say, 'God knows best. He'll help you through this hard time.' Well, God could have stopped it. Why didn't He?
>
> (cited in Froehlich, 2000, p. 125)

'Who can separate us from the love of God?'

I have the confidence to do my work because I have a God who understands suffering: Jesus, who knows human grief, a sense of abandonment, pain, death on a cross; a Father who knows what it is to grieve, to be the wounded healer that writers like Nouwen (1994) encourage us to be, giving sacrificially of ourselves and always with unconditional love and compassion. We seek to imitate the suffering servant, the scarred Jesus in heaven.

Our Jesus is also a resurrected Jesus, a fellow-sufferer who brings the capacity and hope of a new life after death. Hope that this life of pain and suffering is not all there is, and that there is the promise of a place where all this ceases, a place of no more tears for the child and eventually for the family.

One of the main theological reflections that sustains me as a children's hospital chaplain is the redemptive nature of God, and I reflect on this every day. God's nature and will for humankind is redemptive, bringing something good out of what happens. The redemptive benefit of the Christian faith is that I can call the illness or accident evil while believing good can come out of it. But this does not mean I have to conclude that the evil was God's will or is somehow intrinsically good. I name illnesses, accidents, diseases for what they are – not God's idea, will or purpose.

Romans 8.35 says, 'Who will separate us from the love of Christ?' and then lists many really difficult situations. Our challenge is to communicate this truth, that God still loves us, whatever may be happening, and that all these tragedies are just a part of what it means to be human. It is so hard to accept it when you are the one who is suffering, and communicating the redemptive nature of what is happening is something that at times only happens a long way down the line.

'He will wipe every tear from their eyes'

What we can say to families is that after death the children will no longer suffer. This is the promise of Scripture. The commonly used verse for no more suffering for one who has recently died is actually a verse about the end times and the new heaven: 'He will wipe every tear from their eyes. Death will be no more; mourning and crying and pain will be no more' (Revelation 21.4). A family writes, 'Our comfort is knowing that Joshua is at peace now in heaven and our belief that one day we will see him again.'

I do believe in heaven, a place where God is, and hell, a place where God is not, and who gets to go where is the sharp end of our theological reflections. To believe that the words of Jesus apply to the dying child as well as the thief on the cross (Luke 23.43) is both a theologically and a pastorally helpful response. Universalism is a very attractive doctrine when you minister in this type of work – believing that all children, no matter what age or belief, go to be with God when they die. I feel very comfortable speaking of a baby who died at a few days old being in heaven, and this is what I believe. Invariably, my response is to assure the family that their child is safe, in a place where there is no more suffering, no more pain. But should this change for older children?

I have not been comfortable putting an age to when I expect a child to be responsible for owning his or her own faith. One can never be sure of so many factors, such as a child's capacity or exposure to the Christian faith or to how God views him or her. As with some of our theological reflections there are particular differences in this between Protestant and Roman Catholic traditions. The specific nature of heaven and hell is also one of significant theological discussion; currently Wright's (2007) explanation of a new heaven and a new earth resonates with me, but the complexities of the nature of time outside of our earthly existence don't encourage me to offer an unequivocal view to families regarding where their child might be – paradise, heaven, asleep, and so on. This is where what I believe and what I say comes into very sharp focus and brings me to the tension I have found in this type of work.

To live in a place of hope and to possess hope is essential for both the minister and the family: a hope in a God who is loving and cares for the child and the family, who promises to be faithful to them, who will never change. God has entered into a covenant with us and commits himself to love us always. Our hope is based in trust in a God who will bring about justice and shalom. The Christian message is that we can hope for a different future from the place we are currently in. The Christian hope is not one of idly wishing that something will happen, it is trusting in the unchangeable nature of a faithful God, a God who has the power of resurrection so that we have confidence now in eternal life and the promise of heaven.

If it wasn't for our faith we would never have been able to come to terms with what happened to Joshua. Our faith in God has helped us to cope with our loss over the past four years. God was our rock, our firm foundation.

We did use the hospital chapel, especially on the night Kaitlyn died – it is a very peaceful place. Since Kaitlyn was born I feel my faith has been stronger, I feel closer to God and pray to him regularly, I feel he hears my prayers. I did not get angry or feel resentful to God when Kaitlyn died; in fact it brought me closer to him. It brings me comfort to know Kaitlyn is in heaven and that one day I will meet her again.

The longing of the family, and every family, is that God might miraculously heal their child. This did not happen on that day. What I believe was possible to see was the care and love of God present with the family, assuring them that Tabea, although dying, was well and carried within the strong and gentle embrace of God.

Healing and miracles

I heard a story from a survey where the interviewer asked, 'Do you believe in the God who created the whole world, loves every human being and does miracles and heals today?' The person responded, 'No, just the ordinary one.'

Many Christian leaders in church or chaplains in hospital will have had struggles in this area. We will frequently ask ourselves, 'If I had more faith would more children be healed?' I am very careful about what I pray for a child. I will always pray for healing when asked, but I will rely on what I can only describe as a prompting in my spirit. My understanding is this: God is Spirit, and that Spirit speaks to me and I in turn seek to commune with God every moment of every day. Each time I pray I seek to be guided by the Holy Spirit. I cannot say why at some times I pray with more faith or more specifically than at others, except that I seek to be faithful to the revelation God gives to me.

There is being cured, there is being healed, and there are miracles. A cure is when someone no longer suffers from a particular disease, whereas healing is sometimes partial. I understand healing to take place in many ways, and in a hospital it happens primarily through medical interventions. It is crucial for Christians to appreciate that healing via medicine is a gift of God, from the resources of what God has provided for us. A miracle is something that happens outside the usual medical possibilities and for which there is no rational explanation. I do not know why more children are not healed when they are prayed for, but I believe that God can heal, cure and do miracles and I think that the reasons we don't see more are multifaceted. We will pray for healing as part of our work but this is done almost always by request.

When we look at the Bible, we find that it is not only bad things that happen to children; there are examples in both the Old and New Testaments of children being healed and even brought back to life – Elijah, Elisha, Jesus, Peter and Paul all raised people from the dead (1 Kings 17.17–24; 2 Kings 4.17–37; Matthew 9.18–25; Luke 7.11–15; Acts 9.36–42; Acts 20.7–12). I believe that God still performs miracles and have heard stories of people being raised from the dead in other parts of the world. I cannot offer a clear reason why sometimes it appears God intervenes and other times he does not, or why those who receive this intervention do while others don't.

I have very rarely seen anything that I would call miraculous but this story is one example:

In late December 2008, just before Christmas, our four-year-old son James became very ill and was diagnosed with Philadelphia positive acute lymphoblastic leukaemia. We could not believe it – our beautiful son's life in such grave danger. Treatment began immediately at Birmingham Children's Hospital. James seemed to be tolerating his chemotherapy very well, and never once complained. He was missing his reception year at school, but even this did not bother him. Then disaster struck.

On 14 April 2009 he had a terrible reaction to one of the chemotherapy drugs. His condition quickly deteriorated and he was taken to intensive care for initial observation at 4 p.m. By 10 p.m. he was being ventilated and we were being told that he was 'on his last reserves'. We were in total shock and couldn't understand what was going on. His tummy was massively distended and the doctors didn't know why. James was given bag after bag of blood but his blood pressure wasn't holding, suggesting internal bleeding. The next day they opened his tummy and found that his liver had failed (it was pale cream in colour) and he needed a transplant. We were also told that he was just too sick for a transplant – he would not survive the operation.

By now James was on full life support, including kidney dialysis and adrenaline to keep his heart going. They also had to leave his tummy wound open because he was too distended to close in theatre. It then transpired that as well as the drug reaction he had *C. difficile* (a devastating bacterial infection), which explained further the fact that he had, as they described it, total organ failure, including his bowels which were proliferating blood. The doctors said they did not believe he would make it but would carry on with the life support unless they believed it was futile or that James was suffering. Not an hour went by without the doctors and nurses having to deal with a critical event: our son's life was hanging in the balance minute by minute. We kept a 24-hour vigil, praying for a miracle.

We got a miracle, we believe quite literally. We contacted Paul, the hospital chaplain, and asked him if he knew any faith healers. We were so desperate we would have tried anything, and at the very least we thought it would be a comforting experience. Paul said he knew some people. Two wonderful ladies came together and prayed over James: Elsie, a small, quietly spoken lady, and Gloria, an elder of a local church. Before we took them to James's room, Elsie said that she had told her son the evening before that she was coming to pray for a boy at the hospital who had liver failure. Her son had said, 'Mum, I really have a strong feeling that the boy's name is James.' Gloria told us that she had a passage from the Bible going over and over in her mind, and that she had looked it up before coming. The passage was in the book of James. It was as though there were things at play that we could neither know nor understand. The prayers over James did not last long, but we were so comforted and moved by them. We thanked the ladies and they left. That same night his recovery began with his liver healing.

The drugs and machines supporting James's life were gradually withdrawn over the next few weeks, and slowly, slowly, we got our boy back. When they switched off the drugs that had kept him sedated and paralysed for nearly four weeks, that was the hardest part because he was awake but unable to move. All his muscles had wasted away, and he was still ventilated. To see the tears rolling down his cheeks as he tried to speak was heartbreaking.

To our great relief it appeared that he was not brain-damaged. He came out of intensive care and was transferred back to the oncology ward, and since then he has never looked back, eventually coming out of hospital on 3 June 2009 after being away from home for over two months. His strength has been amazing, and day by day he has got better. He had to learn to walk again, and his dad kept up a physiotherapy regime at home. He was off the nasal feeding about a month later, and amazingly was able to walk around Drayton Manor Theme Park on his fifth birthday on 24 July. He is now back at school, full of beans and enjoying life.

When we reflect on this dreadful episode we are absolutely sure that the turning point was Elsie and Gloria's visit. Something changed that day, and James's condition did nothing but improve from that moment on. Indeed, he now has the oncology doctors scratching their heads because, ten months on and with no chemotherapy, he has no detectable leukaemia.

We wish we saw this more often, so how can we explain it? I cannot offer an explanation for this story outside of God, and I need God's gifts of discernment and prompting as much as I need faith to pray for healing and miracles. When all is said and done, we call upon the mercy of God. From reflection on Scripture and experience, it seems reasonable to conclude that healings such as these should be seen as signs of the kingdom rather than the results of faith or saying the right prayer.

Conclusion

When we take Scripture as a whole and all these factors into account I think the God we know, understand and love is the one who is in the hospital bed, in the operating theatre, intimately involved with those who suffer. The God I know does not plan the illnesses and deaths of the children we care for.

Whatever else I think, I believe God is in the midst of suffering. We have a Jesus who has personally known suffering and death. He does not stand on the outside uninterested or disengaged with the dying child or bereaved family; he seeks to come alongside in solidarity. This is one reason why the poem 'Footprints' is so popular: it talks of a God who is with us, supporting and sustaining us. It reflects Immanuel, God with us. We have a trust and understanding that our God promises he will never leave us, so that we can say to families with conviction that God will journey with them, that he will carry them when necessary.

My God can transform suffering (but this needs to be discerned by the family, not the professional). He inhabits suffering, abhors suffering, weeps over suffering. We can explain some but not all of what happens, and this keeps us humble in the face of sickness and disease but confident in the compassion and love of God. We permanently live in this tension.

Theological integrity versus pastoral expediency is another tension I constantly live with. How do I take seriously the faith I believe in and respond to the pastoral situation before me? Does what I say match what I believe, or perhaps what I believe most? For instance, when discussing heaven with the family of a teenager, I do believe in places with and without God but I also believe in being kind, gentle and compassionate and seeking to bring comfort to those in deep distress. But what belief gets manifest in my pastoral care? I confess that sometimes compassion is expressed over other biblical truth I may believe. What theological cost am I willing to pay to buy pastoral comfort? The question becomes: is this in effect good theology because I seek to offer compassion?

We can be tempted to seek to explain questions that families are not asking, or fail to be discerning in our listening to what is really being said. It sounds like a question, but is it rhetorical: when and how does it need to be engaged with? I stayed up all night with one father once. His child was dying and he wanted to discuss all the ins and outs of what might happen to that child. Where was God and how could he make sense of this tragedy? He leaned one side of the cot and I leaned the other and we talked for hours – they were his questions, his timing, his pace. I had not dreamed this was what he wanted or needed to do hours before his child died. He thanked me for my time and I sought to console him the next day when his child died.

I encourage all carers to aim for a thought-through, thoughtful faith that engages with the tough questions without triteness or running away, a faith that embraces mystery and asks 'What we do know about God?' We can serve in this type of work without theological embarrassment, looking the family and other professionals in the eye and saying that God cares passionately for this child and family. There is a saying which I find very helpful: 'The truth is the truth whether you believe it or not.' I content myself with an equal belief in the concept of absolute truth and my ability to never know it all this side of heaven. I recognize I do not a have a complete and irrefutable answer to some of these questions, but my theology gives me a quiet confidence in:

- a loving God, who cares for sick and dying children;
- a God who seeks to offer the balm of comfort, peace, hope, strength and redemption to those who suffer, and the promise of an eternal life with no more suffering;
- a God who calls his people to imitate his care and has promised to give us the resources we need to do this work as we sacrificially presence ourselves with those who suffer.

For reflection

- Have you ever presented an incomplete or unhelpful understanding of God and the Christian faith in the context of a dying child or a bereaved family?
- What might you want to teach differently next time?
- What do you need to remember about the nature of God to take with you into caring situations?
- Can healing be through not being healed?
- Where do you have a tendency or temptation within theological integrity and pastoral expediency?

3

Preparing to care

> Some people come into our lives and quickly go.
> Some people move our souls to dance.
> They awaken us to a new understanding
> With the passing whisper of their wisdom.
> Some people make the sky
> More beautiful to gaze upon.
> They stay in our lives for a while,
> Leave footprints on our hearts
> And we are never the same again.
>
> (Flavia Weedn)

> Alexandra Lister was born 9 May 2005 but quickly became known by her middle name, Willow, because Emily (her elder sister – aged two) couldn't pronounce Alexandra correctly. She very nearly died in the first 24 hours with a major heart abnormality that hadn't been previously diagnosed. Willow had been born with Charge Association – a distinct group of debilitating problems affecting one in 10,000 babies. She was quickly transferred to BCH and underwent several operations, including the insertion of a tracheostomy tube which enabled her to breathe unaided. During this time we were approached by an Anglican minister in the ITU [intensive therapy unit] who showed great concern for our daughter. Although this was our first contact with the hospital's chaplaincy, scepticism was soon replaced by warm reassurance as Nick became a dependable presence in this strangely sanitized world. While assorted medical professionals – nurses, senior clinicians and the cardiac liaison sister – would all communicate to us on a professional level, only the minister seemed completely detached from this medical jamboree. Having a sick child made us keenly aware of Willow's spiritual welfare and, while not wishing to embrace God wholeheartedly, when confronted with the prospect of losing our child we looked forward to Nick's visits.

In the introduction I described different types of care as what we offer to address the concerns, problems, needs and issues of an individual or family. What is perhaps unique with this type of care or visiting is that often we are offering care not to the one who is ill but to parents and wider families, because the person who is ill is a baby. In offering this care, the sort of issues we may become involved with, directly or through referrals, include:

- religious – rituals, blessings, baptisms and funerals;
- spiritual – questions about death, the meaning of life, suffering;
- pastoral or practical – financial (benefits, etc.), home help, respite care, emotional care, sibling support.

What are we seeking to achieve?

Biblically, psychologically and socially there are a multitude of potential objectives for our caring. Some are obvious, others less so. One way of looking at this is to take the Bible passages that talk about how we relate to one another as a basis for seeking to imitate God in our religious, spiritual and pastoral care:

- Love one another: John 13.34, 15.12, 17; Romans 12.10; 1 Peter 1.22.
- Care for one another: 1 Corinthians 12.25.
- Accept one another: Romans 15.7.
- Be kind to one another: Ephesians 4.32.
- Be compassionate to one another: Ephesians 4.32.
- Serve one another: 1 Peter 4.10.
- Bear one another's burdens: Galatians 6.2.
- Be hospitable to one another: 1 Peter 4.9.
- Pray for one another: James 5.16.
- Be concerned for one another: Hebrews 10.24.
- Aim to do good to one another: 1 Thessalonians 5.15.
- Comfort one another: 1 Thessalonians 4.18.
- Bind up the broken-hearted: Isaiah 61.1.
- Comfort those who mourn: Isaiah 61.2.

Within palliative care and bereavement care there are many opportunities to care for and serve others, and these passages can give us an insight and inspire us in particular situations.

A journey together

Preparing to care is about getting ready to set out on a journey. Some of the meanings I derive from the idea of journeying together include:

- recognition that no one is alone
- companionship
- a sense of movement
- a sense of direction
- an emphasis on travel, not arrival
- not necessarily knowing what comes next or what is around the corner.

For some people it can be helpful to use a metaphor as it gives an insight into the relationship that you are offering.

Theological model

Our ministry can be very Christological – some might describe it as incarnational – seeking to be present, to be human, to accompany the families we seek to serve. To genuinely imitate an incarnational model of ministry of care is to be present but also to be interventional. To be incarnational is not a passive role but a proactive model: to intervene, speak out and up, advocate, and sometimes, as Jesus did (and still does today), take the first step as well as responding to requests, presentation of needs and questions. To offer sacrificial availability, to come with nothing in our hands, to families who often feel powerless, is a powerful gift. We seek to serve and not be self-seeking or serving. Our work must always be gracious and generous, This is especially true when relating to families who have been accused of harming or neglecting their children. I have been in this situation more times than I care to remember, and for some people this is an unforgivable, incomprehensible sin. The ministerial way forward I have found is to first give the accused the benefit of the doubt: they are innocent until proven guilty. Second, they are still the parents; and last, if they did do it they need help, and if they did not do it and are being falsely accused they need help. To be non-judgemental is a virtue to strive for and for which we should draw upon every Christ-like strand of generosity we can muster.

Preparing to care: for everyone's SAKE

I have developed SAKE as a framework for those training to work in palliative care:

- Skills
- Attitudes
- Knowledge
- Ethics.

Skills

Being present and available

We can never overestimate the power of just being present. Being alongside can be beneficial. When I explain this to students, sometimes I will put it like this: 'Being present is sometimes all I have.' Some are shocked that this so-called experienced senior chaplain, who leads a multi-faith team at BCH, has not got any more words of wisdom besides 'Be there.' We cannot overestimate the level of support a family can feel when we come alongside them in these times. It may well be that you are the only person they know who they feel comfortable talking to; it may well be that you are the only person who appears comfortable seeing their child, given how ill the child looks and the number of machines he or she is linked up to. We go into situations as pastors, we seek to create a safe place where families can explore their emotions, questions and issues. Musgrave and Bickle call presence 'active silence' (2003, p. 67); this is a helpful term and insight in joining up our key objectives.

Encouraging active listening

Active listening is central in many pastoral care training courses. This includes appropriate body language and other signs that show people that we are really listening. I use the term 'compassionately professional' to describe how I try to engage with families. I am also aware that there can be a fine line between coming across as interested and appearing nosey!

The sin of multitasking is prevalent in our society. It is vital when we care to give our entire attention to the task at hand. This may also involve listening to what the Holy Spirit is saying to us but it certainly shouldn't include planning our evening meal or responding to a text message. We need to demonstrate empathy and a heart of compassion which comes through in our response. We need to be interested in what people are telling us, encourage them to talk and realize that talking and crying are therapeutic. Sometimes it will be painful to listen, particularly when this evokes memories or feelings in ourselves that are hard to handle, but it is a sacrificial gift that we can offer to others. We need to be and provide a safe place and time where people can let go and confront their feelings and thoughts. We also need to be prepared to reflect back to others some of what we see and hear: for example, to help them move beyond self-pity. We may also find that we ourselves are comforted or supported by the child, young person or family in palliative care or bereavement.

One of our tasks is to listen to the God others are revealing. As I mentioned in Chapter 2, my praxis is to be aware that I take God with me and seek to find God where I am. I am always prepared to find a new fresh revelation of God among the dying and bereaved.

We also need discernment as to what is going on with people. Sometimes the family will stop going to church. In talking to them, it may emerge that it is not God they are trying to avoid, but rather the well-meaning people at church who do not know how to relate to them or who relate in a way which is less than helpful. It is important also to hear the voices of the bereaved and allow them to share their feelings and perceptions of what has happened to them. A mother said to me, 'I do feel immense grief and loss, and I long to hold my baby in my arms again. But underneath and through and over all that, I feel immense joy. I was given the gift of my baby, and there are not words enough to express how precious he was to me and how great a gift he was.'

Helping make some sense of bad news

Sometimes I meet families whose children appeared perfectly healthy one day and the next they were in hospital with a poor prognosis. Part of what I do is help them process the bad news. In writing 'make some sense of bad news' I am perhaps reaching for the impossible; sometimes there is no sense, no logic, no justice, and it can help to say so.

Bringing appropriate hope

We must make a commitment to be and bring appropriate hope to the family – not just a fallback in the future hope of the Christian, but a hope that has some reality in the present, too. We must never be glib or raise false hope.

Helping children die well

Part of what we seek to do is to help children die well. This means different things in different contexts depending on age, capacity, etc. But what is usually involved is enabling the family to say goodbye, to communicate love and to try and make sure there is nothing unsaid or unfinished.

Facilitating requests for rituals

Some families will want some sort of ritual as their child is dying. Sometimes this is baptism but it can also be a blessing or some sort of spiritual or religious 'send-off'. This can facilitate families saying goodbye, and the person enabling them can sometimes give guidance or suggestions or encourage acts that demonstrate feelings. An example of such a ritual is given in Chapter 9.

Facilitating forgiveness

As mentioned in Chapter 2, for some grieving parents forgiveness is a significant issue. There may be a need to forgive others or even God, or to ask for forgiveness for their sins which they feel may have contributed to their child's illness. Parents who have children against medical advice or whose behaviour while pregnant had an impact on their unborn child may be in this category. When children die through an accident, sometimes parents will blame themselves and wonder what they could have done to prevent it. I have grown in my appreciation of a minister's unique position in facilitating access to forgiveness for him- or herself, others or God.

Keeping the name alive and honouring the family

'Please keep the names of our children alive by talking about them.' I heard this said by Peter Griffith at a conference on child bereavement. I use the name of the child as often as I can, especially when he or she is dying. We find that reading names out at events like memorial services is very powerful. We have a wonderful opportunity to honour the child from outside the family unit, and I think this makes it even more of a blessing to the family. We will often have had contact with the child and family before they move to palliative or bereavement care, and can talk about the child and identify some of his or her positive characteristics. Our secretary, Wendy, received a phone call from a bereaved mum and greeted her with, 'Oh, Adam's mum.' The mum was overjoyed and tearful that her son was remembered by name.

Being both proactive and reactive

Effective holistic care should have two facets. One is reactive: it is important for people to have places and people they know they can call on. The other is proactive: sometimes we need to initiate opportunities for care – in meeting people, providing services, laying on events, offering support and prayer.

I suspect many of us have a default in this area and are more comfortable being either reactive or proactive in pastoral situations. Many of us are not comfortable just waiting around for people to realize they have a problem, nor are some of us comfortable intervening.

Being able to work within appropriate boundaries

All religious, spiritual and pastoral care should be undertaken within an understanding of appropriate boundaries. Clearly, in a hospital or hospice there will be guidelines as to what is appropriate or not, but in a church context it can be helpful to discuss boundaries and to know our accountability and referral structures.

Attitudes

Desire to build genuine relationships

This is key to effective caring. It is a skill that can be learnt, but must first be an attitude. We need a desire to really help people, and this can be risky in palliative and bereavement care. We should be prepared to be there for the long haul.

Do not feel you have to have all the answers

'I don't give answers, I seek to be present' (Roman Catholic sister). If we can really have this attitude towards our own role and function when relating to children and their families, we will save ourselves from unnecessary stress and resorting to platitudes. We will pick up on the temptation of rescue and rescuer later.

Be comfortable around death

It may seem an obvious thing to say, but to engage in palliative and bereavement care you need to be comfortable around death. This may mean that first you need to process some of your own feelings or experiences to ensure that you avoid projecting your own problems on to those you are seeking to support.

Don't take control – unless it is given

Having an attitude of service is vital. We are there to serve the family's needs, not to take over. Although there may be times when we are asked to take control of a situation on behalf of the family, as much as possible we should seek to empower and facilitate and advocate rather than overpower or domineer.

Be open to the unexpected and non-judgemental

We should have an attitude of openness as people's responses to dying and death can be so varied, and we need to be able to be non-judgemental and accepting of the way in which people behave at times of great stress and strain.

Knowledge

Self-awareness

Many of us work instinctively or intuitively, but this makes it more difficult when we try to explain how we approach pastoral care in our context or in training others to do this work. I know that who I am is significant in the way I care, and in the families who most readily relate to me. We need to ask ourselves: where are our weaknesses, strengths, places of vulnerability, blind spots, default positions, assumptions, presuppositions? Knowing all these will help us be more effective carers.

Knowing when to offer different types of care: religious, spiritual and/or pastoral

In the introduction I gave examples of how I used religious, spiritual and pastoral care with one particular child. We need to be able to identify which is appropriate in our context. For example, we may alienate some by offering religious care when their major need is pastoral, whereas others can be frustrated by what they see as woolly spirituality when what they want is a clear, biblically based response. We also need to know which type of care we feel equipped to offer. If we are uncomfortable or feel ill equipped to deal with deep theological questions, then we need to draw in others who are happy talking at this level. If what is needed is a hot meal, don't spend lots of time talking – do something practical!

Understanding family structure and dynamics

Pastoral care of families experiencing the palliative care of a child or bereavement may well be stressful and tiring to the caregiver. Caring one-to-one is hard enough, but then in moving on to another member of the family we have to change gear or maybe start again, and this all takes energy. It can be helpful to talk directly to siblings and to continue to talk directly to the child even if the parent answers. Be prepared to persevere in building relationships and be sensitive to family dynamics and tensions; try not to appear to take sides. We may also need to be prepared to intervene if we see something that really causes us concern, but it can often be helpful to take advice first. Sometimes just taking someone off for some space can be helpful. We should also know the referral options if people need care for issues that are more complex or require professional intervention. We may also need to be aware of the implications of some of the medical conditions encountered, as there could be future implications for the family.

Research suggests that there are three areas where things can go wrong when a child is ill:

- *Withdrawal and isolation* A parent or sibling may 'shut down' and not be able to engage in family life as usual. If this goes on too long it can become very disruptive.
- *Hostility* Some family members may seem angry a lot of the time, with other family members bearing the brunt of this anger.
- *Seeking secondary gains* Some family members may feel that the child's situation merits special attention from others, particularly if it is as the result of an accident or was recent in onset. This can result in a focus on the illness or disability, with the family's needs to continue to function being ignored.

(Adapted from Power and Orio, 2003, pp. 61–2)

Understanding different types of death

As I have talked with nurses, I have found that the general consensus from their observations is that sudden death is more difficult as it takes away the opportunity to say goodbye. This is not to say the other way is easier, but this factor of preparing for goodbyes – or, if you like, a good death – is an essential concept to engage with. By a good death I mean one where pain is well managed, where there is time for everyone to say goodbye, where an end-of-life ritual, if wanted, can be conducted, and where anything needing to be said is said. A long-term illness can be a real strain on the family, relationships, siblings and finances. But there are opportunities to prepare for the death and say goodbye properly, whereas with a sudden death there may be no opportunity to say goodbye, with all the regrets this may bring.

One of the aspects of a family in palliative care is that loss and therefore grief starts sometimes a long time before the death of a child. One family we supported had a child with problems at birth that had not been picked up on scans. They realized soon after birth that something was wrong, and it soon became apparent this was serious. When they were told the illness was terminal they obviously went into shock. This is when the strong sense of a loss of hope for the dreams for the child quickly manifested itself. It seemed to me, as someone supporting them, that although they were grieving the imminent bereavement, the loss of future seemed equally powerful.

'My whole world collapsed in a instant,' said a mother on hearing her daughter had been killed in a car accident. When we think of the different ways children die, we are also struck by how many cannot be planned – traffic accident, fire, brain haemorrhage, undetected problems on a scan, cardiac arrest, murder, suicide. Some of the stories in this book are from families whose children have died under such circumstances. They may have feelings of regret; perhaps the last time they spoke was not ideal, or they had not seen each other for a while. Complex family structures add to the difficulties. Blame is another factor that comes into play, blaming self and others as well as God.

Michael Dunn raises an important issue for those left after a suicide. Research has shown that there may be ill feeling from others towards them; there may be some disquiet, similar to their own, that they must have contributed to the death in some way. He says, 'There's nothing we can do about this except to be more alert in the future to others' needs who might be in our situation' (cited in Hurcombe, 2004, p. 132). It is important that we create honest pastoral dialogue, support structures and rituals to support families no matter how their child has died.

Ethics

Seek to be a virtuous carer

To some, 'virtuous' may seem an old-fashioned word, but virtue is a helpful lens to employ. A virtue is a positive characteristic; it is about the type of person I want to be, not just what I want to do. As a carer of vulnerable people I want to be gentle, courageous, compassionate, honest, respectful . . . You may have other qualities you want to add. We may be more anxious about what we say and do around children and their families, but first, who we 'are' is more important and will shine through all we 'do', good or bad.

Do not play games

A dilemma we face in any pastoral work is the capacity for people to play games or encourage us into games or roles that we want to resist. One of the most common is the drama triangle that is found in Transactional Analysis theory. There are three psychological positions that can be adopted: victim, rescuer and persecutor. People tend to take on these roles as a defence mechanism, to avoid either conflict or personal responsibility. Those involved in the triangle (see Figure 3.1) adopt a position according to what is happening at the time. It is easy to see how someone whose child is dying or dead can feel like a victim, and will either give off signals that encourage rescuing or will turn into a persecutor when trying to find someone to blame for what has happened.

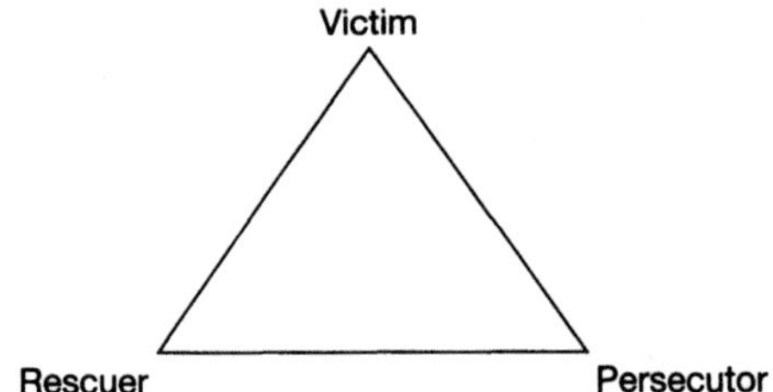

Figure 3.1 The victim–rescuer–persecutor triangle

Taking on these roles can be tempting to the carer too. However, we should always strive to act ethically, particularly when we find ourselves in situations like those in the next two sections.

Seek to facilitate and empower

It is very easy to get drawn by the families into decisions that need to be made. These could be about withdrawal of treatment, organ donation, cremation or burial. I understand why families desire some help or advice and it is tempting to give our opinion, but this is something I shy away from for the following reasons:

- We are in danger of disempowering the family.
- It is not our decision to make.

- We could end up siding with one side of the family.
- What about later on, when the family disagree with us?

I find that the best practice is to help the family process their dilemma. I will take them through the options and the pros and cons and do my best to help draw out their preference.

Accept that you cannot make everything right

When discussing how ministers might help, Louisa's mum, Sharon, says we cannot make it all right:

> You can't, but that's okay. I'll never find a reason why she died, but there is a reason why she was alive, but it is not yet all clear why. It is hard enough, you drive yourself mad finding an answer, a reason. But this is hard.

I find these words from Louisa's mum very helpful and liberating. It is very tempting for us to come and sort out the problem: every serving bone in our altruistic body can shout out to help them make sense of their situation and pain and offer answers and antidotes. Sometimes we have to acknowledge that there are no immediate answers, no balm that is appropriate to the magnitude of the grief. I find this position very threatening to my justification of being present. Surely I should have an answer – that's my job.

Underpinning all of this is the need to build healthy relationships avoiding an over-reliance or dependency on us as carers.

The roles we can play

Validator – it's okay to feel like that

The mum of the dying child is feeling guilty that one moment she does not want the child to die and then the next this is precisely what she does want, because she cannot bear to see her child suffering and in pain. Most parents in this situation, fortunately, have never been there before and so they have no idea whether what they feel is acceptable. I have been asked, 'Is it natural to feel like this?' It is helpful to be able to say yes. Sometimes they do not put it into words, but you sense that they are unsure. So we have learnt to comment: 'It is okay to feel like that, you know. It's the most natural thing in the world.'

This leads us to the next role.

Discerner – where is wisdom?

We need to be able to discern what is going on in a situation so we can try and offer the appropriate response. Sometimes we can ask outright; sometimes we need to discern, from what is being said, what is real and what is perhaps a transient thought that the person then regrets or realizes doesn't reflect what he or she really thinks. We may also want to use tools to help us in this discernment process, and in Appendix 5 is an 'attitude to grief' scale that may enable us to explore grief with someone (however, such tools do need to be used by people who have the appropriate level of skill).

Conversation partner – 'How's today, your child, the food?' 'Has anyone visited?'

Although I advocate silence in some encounters with families, at the beginning of many meetings we do need to be able to make conversation so people relax and are comfortable with our presence. I spend a reasonable amount of my time talking about the children's or family's interests, sport, hobbies, the wider family, etc.; it is sometimes difficult to talk about current events as the families may not have had a great deal of opportunity to watch the news or read newspapers. Even if this type of conversation does not go any further or deeper, it is an expression of pastoral care.

I wonder if this is more difficult for introverts than extroverts; if so, some self-awareness can be helpful. If all else fails there is always the weather!

Advocate – how can I help?

Sometimes a family may not be getting the service they feel they need but don't seem to be getting anywhere with attempts to access it. It may be necessary to support a family by speaking to the local health authority, hospital or hospice. This can sometimes seem like a daunting prospect, when you don't know who to call or how to approach the provider. The family may specifically ask you to intervene for them; while this would be appropriate in some circumstances, in others professional help may be the way to proceed. Within the healthcare system there is an understanding and sometimes commitment to provide a service that acts as an intermediary, an advocate, to present the needs of the family to the Trust. Patient advisory and liaison services in hospitals should be able to advise families regarding this.

We can only go so far

We need to remember that we are not counsellors yet we give counsel, and are not gatekeepers but may be perceived as holding some keys. Within these constraints some counselling skills may be useful, for example these key elements of a narrative approach suggested by Machin:

- listening to the client's story (external narrative);
- exploring the unsatisfactory (painful) aspects of the story (internal narrative);
- finding a more satisfactory (meaningful) story (reflexive narrative);
- absorbing the new meanings of the story into the wider life of the client. (2009, p. 114)

Temptations in caring

Pastoral expedience

Theological integrity versus pastoral expediency is a place I frequently live in. This can happen when I am asked questions such as 'Where is my little boy now?' or 'She's an angel with God, looking down on us, isn't she?' The temptation to become complicit is enormous. What should we do, what should we say? Do we have any certainty around what we believe anyway? There is also a danger of colluding with people, where we go along with what they are saying because we don't want to upset them or cause conflict. Occasionally there may be a good pastoral reason for this but generally we should be wary of being trapped into acting in ways which we later think are unethical or unhelpful. I find myself asking: how do I take seriously the faith I believe while responding to the pastoral situation before me? Does what I say match what I believe, or perhaps what I believe most? I confess that sometimes compassion is expressed over other biblical truth I may believe. What theological cost am I willing to pay to buy pastoral comfort? The question becomes: is this in effect good theology because I seek to offer compassion?

Pat answers

The temptation to come out with platitudes when comforting bereaved families stems from good and varied reasons. However, we must be aware of where these desires come from and the effect they can have on the situation. Sometimes we can have an overwhelming desire to say something that comes from a need to help, to contribute, even to rescue others in their feelings of drowning. We may want to empathize and identify with their pain, and the temptation is to murmur, 'I know.'

To find meaning in death is one of humanity's greatest needs, especially with a child dying before its parents. But this should not lead us into the world of trite comments. A mother recounts her own experience:

> And yet when this [baby] dies, everybody acts like it's nothing: 'Oh well, better luck next time'; 'It's better he died before you got to know him';

> 'You'll have more babies'... So parents who lose a baby will generally try to hide their feelings of grief from others for fear of ridicule, disapproval, or stern lectures about how lucky they are – to have other children or the ability to have new (and obviously improved) babies.
>
> (Klass, 1996, p. 203)

Giving in to expectations

Some of us tend to end up being crippled by our own expectations when we fail to act as we hoped or intended. Others of us feel the weight of the expectations of others and become discouraged by feeling that we never do quite enough. Also, we can shoulder too much responsibility ourselves – responsibility that either belongs to others or is God's. Some of us feel over-responsible for others and this can lead us to act in ways that are disempowering and ultimately not helpful. We should feel an appropriate responsibility but not a heaviness.

One of the early temptations I used to have was to move to victory too quickly. I wanted to remind people that their child was in a better place and that the pain would get easier. I think this came from my own sense of unease in situations and not wanting to feel defeated. Looking back, I can even spot elements of wanting to remind families that they must not forget the victory of the cross and should remember that death is not the end. That was a premature preaching of good news to the poor. This poem from the Northumbria Community reflects an antidote to our temptations:

> Do not hurry as you walk with grief
> It does not help the journey.
> Walk slowly, pausing often.
> Do not hurry as you walk with grief.
> Be not disturbed by memories that come unbidden.
> Be gentle with the one who walks with grief; if it is you,
>   be gentle with yourself.
> Swiftly forgive, walk slowly, pausing often.
> Take time to be gentle as you walk with grief.

I do not think this is a licence for prolonged indulgent grief, but a reminder that the grievers need to be kind to themselves and not feel they need to 'snap out of it'.

Should we ever challenge?

Very occasionally I feel the need to challenge. Sometimes this is prompted by God, and other times I observe something that concerns me, such as a neglect or treatment of siblings that I think may be damaging to them. This story picks up our previous two themes:

> The Master always left you to grow at your own pace. He was never known to 'push'. He explained this with the following parable.
>
> 'A man once saw a butterfly struggling to emerge from its cocoon, too slowly for his taste, so he began to blow on it gently. The warmth of his breath speeded up the process all right. But what emerged was not a butterfly but a creature with mangled wings.
>
> 'In growth,' the Master concluded, 'you cannot speed the process up. All you can do is abort it.' (de Mello, 1985, p. 167)

Mixed motives

A counsellor I work with often asks me, 'For whose benefit did you do that?' This simple question cuts me to the quick and encourages me to examine my motives, which can range from wanting to make myself feel better – or useful or helpful – to making others feel better. The bottom line is, 'Did I do it for the well-being of the family?' Although I do not personally believe it is possible to do any action from a wholly 100 per cent altruistic motive, this kind of question will keep us honest. Discernment with patience and compassion must be our watchwords as we explore our motives in preparing to care.

Power

We should be aware that there are power dynamics at play in any pastoral visit and we should not abuse our trust. It can be really helpful to think through such things as appropriate touch and when to ask permission to do something rather than assuming it is acceptable. We need to consider words such as 'equipping', 'facilitating', 'supporting' and 'empowering' rather than 'taking over', 'doing it all', 'being in charge'. We somehow must be what the family needs but in a liberating, not debilitating, way.

Fear

Most of us involved in caring have some level of anxiety or worries about what we may find or how we will cope when we visit a family. This can be rational, as the unknown can seem scary, and the calculated assessment about what we are likely to find should give us some concerns, as experience tells us this is going to be difficult. I think the criteria for the level that we feel and are affected by our fears are threefold:

- Is this fear irrational?
- Does it debilitate us?
- Does it manifest itself unhelpfully in our face-to-face care?

If the answer is no, then accept a level of healthy concern as a sign that you care and are not being blasé or over-familiar. This is the type of issue to discuss with a spiritual director or soul friend.

Caring for carers and self-care

There are similarities between the advice and support we would give to carers and the advice we would do well to take ourselves in this stressful area of ministry. Some of the principles involved will be generic for care in other types of ministry, but many would acknowledge that there are unique pressures, strains and challenges in caring for dying children, their families and bereaved families. It is important to remember that, for all the reasons mentioned earlier and others, this type of work takes its toll:

- It pushes a lot of the buttons relating to why this is hard for families, and indeed for any human being. This type of death does not seem natural; most of the time there are no answers; we feel helpless; the problem cannot be fixed.
- We can regularly be shocked, become upset, feel overwhelmed.
- It can leave us with unresolved questions which cut to the very heart of our work.
- We can get compassion fatigue.
- It is not for everyone.
- We have personal and professional responses. We have different voices, and our head and heart may be saying different things.
- Most of us do not do this work often, so when it does occur we are having to start again in our preparation and gathering of resources.

These are all normal feelings and we need to work out how we will cope and get support in the midst of them. Here are some coping strategies that I have found helpful:

- Be a reflective practitioner and reflect before, during and after the event.
- Debrief and talk to others.
- Don't forget to grieve yourself.
- Be honest with yourself and others.
- Laugh when appropriate: gallows humour can be helpful, but only with appropriate others.
- Be aware of boundaries.
- Use support structures when needed.

In any pastoral work but particularly in this context, we need to be aware of our own strengths, weaknesses and triggers. I am very aware that working with families in palliative and bereavement care is part of my vocation. I have realized that I have become a 'friend of death'; possibly I have always been so. I have never been afraid of death or seeing dead people. I find the metaphor of wrestling helpful in the area of self-care as it encourages me to engage – not the pretend television wrestling but a real grappling with the issues. I have realized that the older the children are, the more personally difficult I find the bereavement. I have sought to reflect on and understand why this is so and have partly concluded that it is because I have formed a reciprocal attachment with them.

The minister and his or her own children

Some carers will have cared for children of a similar age to their children, which may well raise difficult questions and even fears. Others, like me, do not have children and the question I ask is, 'Do I find it easier to do my job because I do not have children?' My considered answer is yes, but since I have nothing to compare my situation to, the question has to remain open. Many ministers who have related to lots of dying children and bereaved families obviously do have children, and there does not seem to be any correlation between the ability to do this type of work and having one's own children. But it is an area where it is important to be self-aware: you need to be prepared for the next time you care for a child who may be the same age as a close relation.

Allowing ourselves time and space to grieve

Although we are professionals in a place of work this does not mean we will not be emotionally affected by what we see, hear about or are involved in. It is a very difficult line we walk as we move between the extremes of being detached or over-involved. Some of the most comforting observations made by families have been when they have seen staff with a tear in their eye. I think this communicates to the family our commitment to the child as well as our own humanity. But we must always be aware of not imposing our grief on others and of dealing with it appropriately. It's a bit like loving people as they need to be loved – what do they need you to be in that situation? Our work does take a natural toll on us and it is essential we look for its signs, some of which may shock us. We have a responsibility to watch out for inappropriate professional and emotional detachment.

I was invited to share in the funeral for a child of a family I knew personally, and as I started to speak I began to blubber like a baby. I really lost the plot: I cried during the whole of my tribute. On reflection I realized that I acted like this as I had gone too quickly into professional mode and had not given myself the permission, opportunity or space to express my own loss. I was on retreat on Holy Island a few days before George's funeral (p. 5) and was aware I had not cried, so I created space by building a stone cairn on the seashore. This was very helpful in connecting with my emotions and grief. Let's remember, it is our humanity that makes us good at our job.

Debriefing

An important aspect within self-care and caring for the carers is the way we deal with helping others process what has happened and how they engaged with the family. Historically this has been by offering a debrief to talk over what has happened. A recent criticism of this has been that we are in danger of re-traumatizing the carer, and it is suggested that instead we discuss what the carer did and affirm what he or she did well. I think this might work in some situations, but there are times when carers will benefit from retelling the story. Appropriate training should be sought before embarking on such support.

A healthy perspective

Another phrase I find resonates with me is McKelvey's: 'Being faced daily with the fact that life is temporary and unpredictable seriously affects the way I live' (2006, p. 217). This is so true. I have observed that I now take some things far less seriously and have a completely different, healthier perspective on what is really important. Sometimes even golf is just a game! The problems in my life are important, but they are all relative to a family I have just left who have just been told their child is going to die within 24 hours.

Self-care – Kathryn Darby's experience

People often remark that working as a chaplain at a children's hospital must be emotionally draining. Attending to the feelings and witnessing the trauma of people in the hospital can indeed be demanding, especially when several emergency situations fall together in one week. There are external things that can be done to restore my own harmony and balance, such as walking in the woods, having a relaxing bath, taking time off, receiving a massage, listening to music, going to lunch with a friend, reading a good book, going for a retreat, cooking a special meal for family or friends, watching a film. I see these things as integral and essential to the whole of ministry, not extras that I might squeeze in if I am lucky.

There are also internal processes which are important to notice. When reflecting on an encounter that has left me feeling particularly disturbed or upset, a phrase I have come up with is 'what is mine, what is yours and what is ours'. Becoming self-aware is about recognizing in myself what the feelings are about and where they come from in order to deal with them appropriately. In any situation of death and loss, there will be my internal story and also the story unfolding before me which I am part of. Our role as a chaplain is to remain emotionally available and present for the person or family who is experiencing their own grief. Keeping one foot planted on the shore while planting one foot in the rushing stream to reach out a hand to the person drowning is one image that I have returned to. There is little value in jumping in entirely and drowning with the person. I think that one of the ways that we keep one foot firmly on the shore is through an ongoing pilgrimage of self-awareness. Reflecting on our own emotions, reactions and responses, and our own relationship with grief and loss, through journalling, talking with a trusted supervisor or spiritual director, conversation with peers and prayer develops self-awareness.

One of the most significant experiences in my life was the death of my mother when I was 17 years old. C. S. Lewis's description of bereavement rings true for me:

> With my mother's death all settled happiness, all that was tranquil and reliable, disappeared from my life. There was to be much fun, many pleasures, many stabs of Joy; but no more of the old security. It was sea and islands now; the great continent had sunk like Atlantis.
>
> (Lewis, 1978, p. 23)

As a teenager I buried a lot of the grief within and carried on doing the things that teenagers do. Many years later, as a young mother, living in a country far from Canada where I had been born and raised, that grief which I had packed neatly away was suddenly urgent and pressing. Grief has been talked about as something we experience in stages, sometimes overlapping and in no particular order. Another helpful metaphor for me has been a circling back, a revisiting of the initial hurt, which lands me in a new place, generally in a forward direction. Sometimes that revisiting can be dramatic and cathartic. Gradually with time and often through the support of others there is healing and growth. But the journey through grief is a lifetime's work. Conversations, encounters, watching a film or reading a book can suddenly connect me again with my own grief. While there is growth and change, and certainly the rawness is rarely present in the way that it once was, there continues to be a circling back.

When we visit others in their grief, we are wise to be aware of 'what is mine, what is yours and what is ours'. I acknowledge that feelings can rarely be disentangled in any neat order, but ongoing work can be done on self-awareness. Self-care is about honouring the feelings and journey that are personal as well as honouring the grief that essentially belongs with someone else. Looking after myself becomes part of the care I can offer others. Recognizing my own grief, which is separate, is a way of freeing myself to be more available to another person in his or her unique experience. Combined with this is the grief which is 'ours'. Travelling alongside and getting to know children and young people who are dying leads me inevitably to mourn for them and with their families. It is one of the privileges and the costs of becoming involved.

Connecting our theology and our pastoral care

Much of this chapter will have resonated with elements from the previous chapter. Some will have been obvious, some less so. I want to join up a few dots and connect my theology and practice.

Availability and vulnerability are the values of the Northumbria Community. Although they are not designed specifically for bereavement, I have found them very helpful in giving me a focus for what I am seeking to be. They are prefaced by the value of being intentional in them, which makes them come alive even more for how I want to be and how I want my pastoral care to be. I like the simplicity of them; they are easy to remember but difficult to do. They raise the bar to save me from just turning up and going through the motions. To make myself intentionally available to a dying child is to let my protective distancing down. I seek for my theology and pastoral care to be:

- reflective
- gracious
- sacrificial
- liberative
- empowering.

It is an interesting reflection on my journey, of what has influenced what. My tradition would tell me that my theology should shape my practice. This is what I seek to do, but not exclusively. If I am honest, my experience of pastoral care of dying children has now shaped my theology. If I am really honest, this is now intentional practice: to theologically reflect as well as apply my theology gives me two hands to do my work. To take the God that I have to engage with the God that I find is an aspect of my faith that sustains me.

Mindfulness

Mindfulness is much more than remembering. Being mindful is about being attentive; it is about thoughtfulness. As we draw together the threads of our way forward for this chapter, let us consider what we may need to be mindful about:

- There will be a spectrum of ages and a variety of relationships to the dying or deceased child.
- It is a privilege to be involved in supporting the family – this is not just hard work or a job.
- It is supposed to be difficult, even sacrificial.
- It is not about our own grief.
- We can find God in the midst of loss and grief.

For reflection

- What aspects of SAKE do you need to develop in your face-to-face caring?
- What are your triggers and temptations? How do you deal with them?
- Do you have a healthy and robust self-care model in place? When was the last time you reviewed this?
- How can you support and train your co-carers to look after themselves and other carers?
- When are you tempted to hurry with grief? What can you do to address this?

4

Palliative care in practice

At the start of Conor's funeral, as the coffin, designed like a Formula 1 car, came into the chapel to the Formula 1 theme music, my breath was momentarily suspended. Although I had been warned, I could not imagine what the sight of a Formula 1 coffin would be like, and there was something magnificent about its sleek finish and grand design. And in a way this helps me to illustrate the reality of working with children and young people who are ill with life-threatening diseases: they are individuals that astonish, amaze and inspire me as I continue to encounter them in my work as a chaplain at BCH, for they are wondrously made. I remember early meetings with Conor on the oncology ward. He challenged me to a game of Scrabble and proceeded to thrash me. This was the tone of our meetings from that point onwards – the glint in his eye which invited me to a duel, and me taking up the invitation. I brought in a game that I thought I could beat him at: Blokus. The first time I took the game to his ward, Conor was having a 'down day' and was sleeping off the effects of the treatment, but the next time I visited he was sitting up and looking around for another challenge. 'This will give him a run for his money,' I thought, as I presented him with this shiny new board and glittering pieces of red, yellow and blue. He mastered the game in one go, although I had the satisfaction of seeing him stretched just a little as he worked out his strategy.

What did I learn from Conor? What were the tears about, the day before his funeral, as I stroked his cold head and said goodbye at Acorns Hospice? As I looked at his face, battle-scarred by his disease but still shining and peaceful in death, images of his exuberant and irrepressible self flashed into my mind. He had passion and curiosity about life – a deep questioning and desire to learn – which he continued to express, even in the midst of a mounting trial. There were things he wanted to do, even in the last stages of his illness, and with the help and support of his family he did them. He understood the principle of embracing life and living fully, and if there was a way that I could help enable that to happen, by playing a game, or sharing a joke, or answering an honest question with an honest answer, I was honoured to be alongside him.

Visiting people and looking for the answering welcome in the eyes of a parent and the permission to be involved with his or her child, I am also listening for the aspects of character in a child or young person which are waiting to be noticed and valued. We can take pleasure, together, in these aspects of their unique selves which need to be celebrated and

> appreciated – and in life, not only in death. Most essentially, it is the quality of our relationships with one another which give meaning and purpose. My final image of Conor is of him with his foot on the accelerator (expressed by my colleague who led the funeral service), travelling beyond us, forging the path, with his usual display of courage and vitality. His presence enhanced my life, and if in some way I also made a connection with him, then we were both enriched. (Kathryn Darby)

In the previous chapter we explored some of the concepts, issues and challenges we need to be aware of before we engage in the ministry of palliative and bereavement care. We will now look in more detail at how, in practice, we can facilitate, advocate and contribute to the multifaceted care of both the child and the family. In this chapter we will do this by considering the practice of palliative care, and in the next chapter we will focus on the practice of bereavement care.

Breaking bad news

A parent is informed by the doctor that there is no more that can be done for the child and that staff will begin palliative and end-of-life care. Few feel comfortable in engaging with another human being about the pain, shock and anguish of a child dying. Fortunately, ministers do not often have to be involved in breaking the sad news, but it still does occur.

Here are some general guidelines to keep in mind. They can also be passed on to parents and anyone else who may be charged with breaking the news to others.

- Do feel free to break the news in your own time.
- Don't be afraid of long silences after breaking the news.
- Do remember that listening can be as important as speaking.
- Do admit if you feel awkward or embarrassed – attempts to cover this up can be misinterpreted.
- Do allow the person you tell – or the person you hear – to respond to you.
- Don't try to steer the conversation away from death; this doesn't necessarily provide comfort and can give the impression that discussion isn't allowed.
- Don't feel awkward if people show signs of being upset or begin to cry; give them permission in word or manner to express their feelings in whatever way is appropriate and natural.
- Don't make offers of help unless you are sure that you can fulfil them.
- Don't pass on the news to anyone else unless this has been agreed.

- Don't start treating the person as helpless and as needing to depend on others for everything.
- Don't treat the person as now being in a new depersonalized zone.

(Adapted from Woodward, 2005, pp. 22–3)

Telling our families about Kofi's condition was hard, having to explain everything. It was not easy when people said to us, 'He'll be okay,' when we knew that this wasn't to be. We had to stay positive, but be realistic. We knew we would have to treasure each day we had with him. People kept saying to us, 'I don't know how you do it,' or 'I wouldn't be able to cope,' but the thing is, no one thinks they are going to have a child who will be different from the 'norm' – when it happens you do just have to get on with it. Kofi kept us so busy, we never had time to think what hard work it was. I believe that anyone would do the same for their child, but unless you have been in that situation it is hard to imagine what life is like.

Children's understanding of death

Children's understanding of death naturally relates to their age and development stage, as Table 4.1 illustrates.

My suggestion is that we should keep these guidelines in mind and be aware of our own discomfort. It is important not to fudge the situation by talking metaphorically of, say, 'sleeping', or by using the illustration of an animal, when it is healthier to use the word 'die'. Very young children do not have the capacity for abstract concepts and look in literal ways. Although we may be seeking to be gentle and kind we can inadvertently put the wrong images into the child's mind: if my brother is 'asleep', what will happen when I go to sleep tonight? I am currently involved in writing some books for young children, and we have been advised that, in dealing with death, we should use the image of a child and the word 'die', explaining that this means the child was too sick to live and has gone to be looked after by Jesus in heaven, where we will see him or her again.

Some family's stories suggest that sometimes children already know or have an inkling that they are dying. Here are two stories that show different perspectives on this issue.

At the age of nine and three-quarters, Tabea became ill, diagnosed with acute myeloid leukaemia (within six days she died). I'm so thankful to know that she knew Jesus. When Ian tested her on a Bible verse one

Table 4.1 The development of children's understanding of death

Age of child	*Cognitive factors*	*Emotional response*	*Physical response*
Infant and toddler	Onset of attachment at about six months. Permanence of death not understood. Ability to conceptualize the word 'death' very limited. Children begin to incorporate small losses into their lives. Children are aware of the adult use of the word 'death'.	Separation anxiety. Yearning and searching for the person who is not there. Expression of sadness short-lived. Blame other people for death. Fantasies about being reunited with the dead person. Rejection of affection from new primary carer.	Bedwetting. Wetting by day. Increased likelihood of viral infections. Disturbed sleep.
Early years	Ability to classify, order and quantify events and objects but unable to give them a rationale. Concepts of life and death established. Understand that the state of death means not breathing or moving, being still, etc. Permanence of death still not established. Stage of 'magical' thinking, e.g. that own thoughts or actions may be responsible for death.	Excessive crying. Unable to control emotions. Poor concentration at school and play. School refusal. Illusions or hallucinations about the dead person – night terrors. Play out death and dying.	Restlessness. Loss of appetite. Tummy ache – psychosomatic illness. Clinging behaviour. Night terrors.

Table 4.1 (*continued*)

Age of child	*Cognitive factors*	*Emotional response*	*Physical response*
Middle years	Able to explain reasoning in a logical way. Realization that death can be applied to self. Permanence of death established. Death understood as an ultimate reality. Confusion about metaphors and euphemisms associated with death, e.g. 'gone', 'asleep', 'lost'.	Anxiety about other people dying. Disturbance in normal behaviour patterns. More in control of emotional responses. Inability to organize and to concentrate. Stealing objects for comfort. Capacity to sustain feelings of sadness for longer.	Aggression. Changed behaviour. Nail-biting. Sleep disturbance. Physical illness.
Adolescent, early teenage years	Abstract thought patterns established. Interest in physical characteristics of death and dying. Questions about how and why. Own theories about what happens at death and beyond. Interest in ethical issues.	Whole range of emotions displayed. Feeling embarrassed about being different. Anxiety about the future, e.g. material possessions, economics. Inability to form lasting relationships.	Eating disorders. Challenging behaviour. Physical illness. Disturbed sleep. Conflict. Risk-taking behaviour. Increased sexual behaviour.

(Adapted from Brown, 2009, p. 12)

day, she said, '"For God so loved the world that he gave his only son, that whosoever believes on him shall not die but have eternal life." I know, you know!' So when Wednesday came and she said, 'I'm going to die, you know,' we tried to say to her that was why she was here in hospital, to try to stop that happening. She just repeated, 'I'm going to die.' (I do believe God in his own way was preparing her to meet him.)

> As parents, my husband and I have made many mistakes during the course of our son's illness. We've been overly soft when a firmer hand was called for. We've been overly firm when a softer hand was called for. One of the biggest mistakes we made, however, concerns the area of trust. It is not that we set out deciding against telling the truth – quite the opposite, we have always been as honest as we can with our children. It's just that sometimes, at the beginning of David's illness, we did not find out the necessary amount of truth. (Burn, 2005, p. 17)

It is important to be aware from the start that parents may not (or may not yet) want a child to know he or she is dying, and that you therefore need to clarify what they wish you to say or not to say. Once that is clear, be yourself and speak normally about everyday things – children can be in palliative care for many months. I always talk to the children, regardless of their age or level of consciousness, on the assumption that they can understand every word I am saying. I believe this is a sign of respect, treating children with dignity.

This becomes very focused in end-of-life blessings. In these blessings I often thank the child for being born, for all that he or she means to the rest of the family, and say, 'You will never be forgotten,' and 'Your name will live on for ever' (this last point especially if there has been a baptism or naming ceremony). I then encourage the family to talk to the child in a similar fashion. This is very emotive, but is most beneficial for several reasons:

- Some members of the family are doing it already.
- It gives a model and, if needed, permission to facilitate communication between the family and the child.
- It begins the process of saying goodbye.

Occasionally a chaplain or minister is called to do an end-of-life blessing for a child but the parent does not want the child to know he or she is dying. This happens to me and my team about once a year. What do you do? It also applies to siblings, friends, schools, etc. – should they be told and, if so, how? There can be no hard and fast rules here, and in each situation a different variety of factors needs to be taken into account. My observation is framed as a question, 'Who is having the difficulty, the parent or the child?' In my experience it seems as though it is the parents who struggle, not only with telling the child he or she is dying, but then with living with the ongoing unimaginable struggle and engagement of the child with the news.

I recall the first time I was asked to do such a blessing. The child was in and out of consciousness and the parents wanted me to do an end-of-life blessing without telling the child she was dying. I struggled, not only in doing such a ritual but with a large part of myself that disagreed with the parents not telling the child. Fortunately, my reflective practice and self-understanding disciplines kicked in and I was able to do what the family requested. On reflection, I felt I did the best thing by the family but not the child. I respected the family's wishes, which is paramount, but wondered about how much the child understood or would have liked to engage with what was going on. My question is: in whose best interest do we make the decision, and what do we take away from the child in not being able to say goodbye, or from the siblings being able to do the same?

Relating to the dying child

Members of the family will have a variety of perspectives and may experience the pressures differently. As for the child him- or herself, specific needs and concerns will vary, depending on age (at all ages symptom relief and pain management is assumed).

Baby

Babies need:

- frequent physical contact (or touching) from primary carers;
- frequent awareness of voices of primary carers;
- normal routines and maintenance of familiar cultural and religious traditions;
- opportunities to play and to interact with family members.

Pre-school

Small children need:

- reassurance that any separation from primary carers is unavoidable;
- communication in easily understood language;
- explanations about care procedures and administration of medicine;
- constant reassurance about love and care from family members;
- help to indicate levels of pain or distress;
- normal routines and maintenance of familiar cultural and religious traditions;
- opportunities to interact with peers and family members.

Five to seven years

Children in this age group need:

- honest responses to questions about life-limiting illness;
- opportunities to communicate preferences, needs, fears and concerns;
- constant reassurance of the love and care of family members, peers and friends;
- help to communicate levels of pain or anxiety;
- access to educational activities and hobbies;
- contact with school;
- opportunities to reflect on achievements and hopes for the future;
- maintenance of familiar routines and cultural or religious traditions.

Seven to nine years

Children in this age group need:

- open and honest responses to questions about the nature and inevitable outcome of their illness;
- opportunities to express opinions, wishes, anxieties;
- constant reassurance of the love and care of key people;
- freedom to make decisions about pain control, symptom relief and care;
- opportunities to express awareness of how family members are responding;
- maintenance of routines and religious and cultural traditions;
- opportunities to reflect on achievements throughout their life, and hopes for the future.

Adolescents and young adults

Adolescents and young adults need:

- opportunities to express fears and concerns for self and family members;
- privacy, especially when undergoing personal care;
- opportunities to maintain autonomy and independence for as long as possible;
- support from peer groups as well as family members;
- involvement in decisions regarding their care, including symptom control and pain relief;
- maintenance of familiar cultural and religious traditions;
- opportunities to reflect on what they have achieved throughout life;
- acceptance and affirmation of sexuality.

(Brown with Warr, 2007, pp. 123–4)

Planning for the death of a child

Death – how and where?

At some stage when a child is in palliative care, the family will be asked where they would prefer the child to die. Whenever possible and feasible, a family with a child in hospital will also be given a choice of where they want their child to die. Of course, this is not always possible but exploring it will be a part of the end-of-life care pathway. The options are home, hospital or hospice, and the issues that may impact this are the availability of such things as local nursing resources, transport and pain management needs. Choice is very important to some families, who can feel out of control with the outcome of the diagnosis of their child, but it also has an adverse effect on others, who can be crippled by any choice, let alone lots of choices. Best practice is to work with the family and give them time to process the choices that are before them.

I would want to honour the request of the family, but it is also important to explore the pastoral and psychological implications of where a child dies. Many families, if given the choice, will want their child to die at home, and it is completely understandable that you would want your child to die at home surrounded by loved ones and a familiar environment. My main concern here is what memories are left in the home, and especially the room, where the child has died. The family will have the everlasting positive and negative memory that this is where their loved one died, and will ever associate that space, room, bed, etc., with that child. While this can be a wonderfully positive memory, most of the families we support will – fortunately – not have had this experience before and will not be able to draw on and learn from past experience. It is a difficult decision, not least because all health and palliative staff will want to facilitate and respect the wishes of the family, and this is not a time where they will want to challenge their decision.

Another observation I wish to make is that dying at home seems to be a preferred option of healthcare workers, and I want to put it in the mind of ministers that they should at least internally ask whether they should be supporting a family in making this decision.

If the decision is for the child to die at home, we need to be aware that although some children's deaths take place in hospital a significant number do occur in the community, so we can be prepared for this to happen.

Planning for some good memories

This might seem an oxymoron, given the circumstances, but if we listen to the stories of the families we see the value of such planning. Shortly after death, hand and footprints are often taken, along with a lock of hair and photos. All these resources would normally be supplied and facilitated by nursing staff and chaplains, but a visiting minister could be involved if the family wish. It is a very sacred time to spend with the child and the family. If this is not offered as a normal service you could suggest it yourself.

Some families create memory boxes for all the keepsakes. I have known families keep things such as name bands (if the child has been in hospital), clothes, certificates, photos, favourite CDs or DVDs, favourite toys and even the last (unused) nappy. Lauren's mum has the hat Lauren wore when her hair fell out, the sympathy cards, a piece of the blanket she was buried with, her toothbrush and a lock of hair. I have also known of parents planning these boxes with their palliative child, and hospices and palliative care services are good at helping with this. These boxes are revisited by parents as needed and bring a helpful link to the family and their child; you may want to refer to the memory box if you know the family has one.

My advice to other parents who may be going through this is to spend as much time with them as you can and never miss a chance to hold your child, or just to look at them. Even if the doctors tell you your child won't make it, demand to hold your child in your arms, or if you are offered the chance, don't pass it up and say no as you will regret it. I nearly said no and my mom said no, you will regret it for ever. And guess what? I listened to her and she was right. Looking back, if I hadn't done it, I'd have regretted it. Also, don't close your feelings off, as easy as it feels to do, as grief always catches up like it did to me. I tried to forget the pain and it caught up with me. I found my help from the nurses and doctors at BCH was amazing. I made memorial books for Kasey-Jayne and it made me feel like a mother and like she was there with me. I kept things she used at the hospital, clothes she wore, in a box. I hope my story and advice can help other parents going through my experience to maybe give them a bit of courage to do things they never thought they would have the guts to do. (Kasey-Jayne's mum)

Having the time and support to help the boys say goodbye to their sister Chloe was vital. Having the right people, the right place and the right things in place helped them through it. The symbols and tokens shared helped this. The boys had time to buy her pyjamas to wear in her coffin. She 'gave' the boys little bunches of forget-me-nots and they gave her small gold hearts (which we got from the resources held by the chaplaincy team at BCH). (Chloe's mum)

Praying for help and healing

Intercessory prayer for sick and dying children is not without difficulty, and I have touched on this in Chapter 2. It raises many questions or issues. If we are looking to stand in the gap, where is the gap? How do we pray? What do we pray? Do we need to know the need or condition to be able to pray very specifically or can we just pray generally?

Different Christian traditions have their own approaches to intercessory prayer. For some it will be praying in tongues, for others it may be more contemplative. Good advice is to pray as you can, not as you can't. In our chapel we have a variety of ways of praying, including prayer ropes, a prayer tree, a prayer book and candles. We never know whether a request for prayer is genuine or is a 'hedge your bets' type request, but we will always pray when asked and most often feel that we are praying out of weakness.

There are several Scriptures, such as 1 Peter 1.17, which encourage Christians to either call out to God for help or invite other Christians to come and support them. Have you ever thought about the process that happens when you pray with others? We may go through a scenario such as:

- What ought I to pray?
- What does the child or the family want to me pray for?
- What do I have faith to pray for?

I have done a lot of thinking, discussing and reflecting about what we can pray as this is one of the mainstays of our work with children and families. The conclusion I have come to is that I can always pray for three things, no matter what:

- peace;
- strength;
- that they will have God's perspective on the situation.

The reflection we have had within our team is that there is an appropriate difference between our internal and external prayers with a family. What I pray to be heard by the family may be different from what I pray within my head and heart. For instance, at some emergency baptisms I may commit the child to God in my internal prayer but may make a judgement that the family have not quite come to that place yet despite the poor prognosis of their child, or if I feel I do not yet know a family very well I may not use the word 'die' or 'death'.

I personally can no longer pray, 'Lord, if it is not your will for this child to be healed . . .' or 'We trust you . . . we know you know what is best . . . we know we will see this child again.' I am concerned about the image of God such prayers portray – it can sound as though he is a God who wills and desires that a child should not be healed, or has decided it's best if the child is not healed. Ethically I can accept that it may not be in the best interests of some children to live with so much pain and disability. But I am not comfortable praying the words to God in front of the family.

Sadly, one of the children I visited early in my post at BCH was the daughter of a couple I knew. She was very ill but not terminal. I had recently come across a song about peace, and found myself singing this song over her as I prayed for her and with her parents. Day after day I would sing over her, 'Peace to you, we bless you now in the name of the Lord, peace to you. Peace to you, we bless you now in the name of the Prince of Peace, peace to you.' I believe I was seeking to minister deep within her spirit.

Hedging your bets

One of the stories our team recalls when we need a little light relief is of a family who asked us to pray for their child. We went to the bedside and prayed, asking for the child to be blessed, and then began to further engage with the family. It was at this point that the family showed us various icons and images that were discreetly placed around the child's bed, going on to explain proudly that they had asked for a prayer to be said at Stonehenge that morning and wasn't that wonderful! It is not unusual for families to try a range of spiritual resources on such occasions, and this where we engage our theological and pastoral integrity and expediency. Our policy in the team would be to neither challenge nor collude. Our reason for this is that we are alongside the families for such a short time that we often do not know them well, and there are more important issues at hand. However, we would intervene if we thought anything was harming the child.

Families' prayers

This selection of prayers, written in our hospital prayer books, gives an idea of how families are praying for their children and provides insight into their faith and theology. The prayers have a variety of purposes.

Asking for God's help

> Lord Jesus, please will you help my son who is in ICU. Please help him for his breathing and care for him. In a couple of days he will have his surgery. Please always be close to him. I know you listen to prayers. We love him very much. Please care and always be close to him. Amen.

> Dear Lord, Grandma, Grandad, please watch over my baby. Please let this hurdle be small, please don't let it be anything major. Let it be nothing. Please I know that you are always taking care of my babies. Please take extra care this time. I love you all and miss you all.

Hope and resignation

> Dear Lord, please help us. We need a miracle. We're told our little girl has around six months to live. It's highly unlikely she'll get the transplant in time, so please help her. If not, please let her go in peace, not in pain. She has suffered enough. Amen.

In case there is a God

> I am not a religious person, but I'm asking you to make my little girl better. She has been in pain for five months. We have been here now three weeks and she seems to get better, then something else happens. She has been unbelievably brave and takes everything thrown at her. Our three children are the most precious things in our lives. Please make Tanya better, I am begging you.

After death

> Dear God, please take my little princess into your arms and take good care of her, you are her father and I trust will be there for us and let her watch over us. She was such a brave sweet old little girl who fought day and night but just couldn't fight no more. Thank you for blessing me with such a beautiful little girl that'll always be remembered and loved.

To conclude this chapter, here is a message that was sent by a stranger to someone who had lost a child:

> Each day in prayer I thank God for the continued unbroken link which we still have with our departed loved ones through Him. We take comfort from the fact that we can indeed talk to God, the One who is caring for them now and beneath whose gentle, tender love and care they are not lost at all but are now safe, truly safe, safe from all harm and suffering. Furthermore, because above all things God is love, it most surely then must follow that someday we'll meet and be reunited with them again.
>
> (O'Shea, 2008, p. 111)

For reflection

- How can you help families process regrets and what help can you offer before, during and after bereavement? (Some of the resources in Chapter 9 may be helpful.)
- Are you clear about what you do feel comfortable praying for and what you don't?
- What age-appropriate activities and support could you offer siblings?
- Are there any training needs arising out of the material in this chapter?
- How might you be able to support local schools and community groups in palliative care?

5

Bereavement care in practice

> Mitchel is and always will be around for ever, just a little differently. For us it doesn't get any easier. This was so difficult to write and for the most of it I have looked at these computer keys through wet eyes and a pounding heart, but that is love and I always want to feel that hurt. Mitchel Lawrence-Birch died 11 days old but he is very much alive in our hearts.

> Our son Dylan died unexpectedly after craniofacial surgery in 2005 aged 18 months. The best advice I could give is to allow yourself to grieve, let all those emotions enter into your heart and mind, let them stay and settle into your bones! The pain is immense and relentless after losing your precious child, but you have to carry on. Life will never be the same again . . . Depression, desperation, anxiety, denial, shock, numbness, these are just to name a few. Healing – where do you start? I spent the early days reading books and visiting a bereavement counsellor; I then ventured on to spiritual healing and reflexology. Nobody tells you that grief affects all aspects of your life, physically, mentally, emotionally and spiritually. I needed support and nurturing on all levels and somehow found the strength to see me through.

The death of a child is one of the most difficult things that life throws at us. I constantly ask, 'How can I make sense of the death of a child?' Should I try and make sense of it? What am I afraid of? What fears do I need to face? No death, no bereavement is ever the same, even if it looks similar or is in the same family. It affects family members differently, too, and we need to be sensitive to a wide range of needs and perspectives. Dealing 'well' with bereavement can prevent further problems, and that is one of the motivations in writing this book: I want more people to be equipped to journey alongside the bereaved with at least a degree of confidence that they have something to offer.

Relating to bereaved families

The bereavement of others is from the same book, but a different chapter. (Louisa's mum, Sharon Moore)

This is a crucial aspect of our care that can bring us a great deal of anxiety. I want to explore some helpful experiences from fellow ministers and from families.

What you can say

- I am so sorry for your loss.
- How is X today?
- How can I help? (Or better, offer specific help).

What not to say

- I know how you feel.
- Don't worry, you can have another one.
- At least you had your child for this long.
- He or she is in a better place.
- God loved your child more, God wanted your child for an angel.
- Time will heal.
- Think how much money you will now save.
- Have you thought about getting a rabbit or a dog?

Other potential pitfalls

- Be wary of telling your own bereavement story.
- Be mindful that you might be the twentieth person to say, 'I am so sorry for your loss.'
- Be liberated – I once heard a bereaved parent say to a group of professionals, 'Don't worry about saying the wrong thing; it cannot be a worse thing than what has already happened to us.'

As a bereaved parent, Hurcombe summarizes her thoughts and advice. There are some similarities with my own, but she adds some other faux pas. Her list of what not to say or do includes:

- Don't quote verses of Scripture such as 'His yoke is easy and his burden light'.
- Don't compare the loss of a pet, however beloved, with the loss of a child.
- Don't use the poem 'Death is nothing at all' (Scott Holland) with the family.
- Don't tell people not to feel guilty or that it's not their fault.
- Don't say how lucky they are that they have another child or children.
- Don't encourage grief substitutes.
- Don't tell people that their child is at peace and that their child's suffering is over at last.
- Don't comment on how well people are doing in such awful circumstances.

- Don't say that keeping busy is the best thing.
- Don't comment that people will soon get over it and be back to their old selves. (adapted from Hurcombe, 2004, pp. 52–3)

She goes on to say,

> You're probably thinking 'But some of these things are true! What can I say that will be appropriate?' and you're right. The list may seem terribly rigid and I've long forgiven and forgotten who said what . . . mostly. The fact is, though, that there are indeed no words, no words, no words. If a word could be a hug, or a song, or a group of like-minded sufferers who understand how we truly feel, and will be there for the long run through thick and thin, well yes. The best words are probably starkly, 'I'm so sorry. I cannot imagine your loss.' (Hurcombe, 2004, p. 53)

It never ceases to amaze me how grateful families are even when things do not go well. As one family said, 'We would just like to say a big thank you to the minister for all the help and support that he gave to us on the night Joshua died.'

A chaplain's approach – Penny Sherrington, a chaplain at Great Ormond Street

I do a lot of listening. Body language which is not hurried or trying to find answers (there are none); simply being there is important. The ability to be silent is very important. I sat for a hour beside one family whose daughter had died; my being there enabled them to think their thoughts, but they were not alone. There is a similarity with Jesus asking his disciples to watch with him. I am also aware when I may need to go out and let them be alone for a while, with the promise I will come back. Oftentimes I am simply in the room and gently being beside one member of the family; other times I help the family, as when the mum was sitting on her own after the child had died and no one sat next to her, and I gently suggested to the boyfriend that he sat next to her. So much is about not leaving them alone but being sensitive. I also offer some rituals, a candle in the chapel, singing a nursery rhyme that the child likes. The question I am most asked is not 'Why did God let my child die?' but 'What have I done to deserve this?' I always affirm: nothing, it is simply the fragility of life. If I am asked 'Why did God let my child die?' I say that the child's body could not sustain life; he or she was too poorly. There are no answers, and being 'real' is all-important – people sense when you care. At the time they probably won't remember what you say, but rather how you were.

Insights from parents on what helps

Sometimes just being there helps, offering support, and someone to talk to who is being realistic and not just saying things to make people feel better like 'It will be okay' or 'Things will be fine' when that isn't the case. I used to hate it when people said to me, 'Oh you poor thing,' etc. I found this quite patronizing and wished people wouldn't say things like that.

Helping with the practical things after a bereavement, e.g. getting food shopping in, taking or collecting children from school – I needed some time before I felt I could cope with those types of things. The general offers of help are not as helpful as more specific offers – a general offer of 'I am here if you need anything' I did not find helpful, as I was reluctant to ask for help, but if someone said, 'I will go and do your shopping for you,' etc., I was happier about that.

Do call round on your friend or neighbour. There is a feeling of isolation and loneliness after a child has died and the initial attention from family and friends has receded.

Don't be afraid to talk about the deceased child, and don't be afraid if the parent cries or if you cry as well – we want the memory of our child to live on.

Say they are in God's arms, safe with God. I am not sure I found it helpful being told my child had died and was risen with Christ – resurrection wasn't what I asked for.

It helped to be reassured that Cameron was no longer in pain and therefore was better where he is now. This helped because as a mother I always want what's best for my child, and so if I could feel that what had happened was some way better for Cameron, even though it was unbearable for me, then that made me feel a bit better sometimes. Even now, three years on, I still tell myself this and it does help me.

My best friend sat and listened to me however long I talked (and cried) for and didn't mind when I would talk through the same things over and over again on many occasions. Just being able to talk through things with a friend helped me so much. I did have bereavement counselling as well, but I know I wouldn't have got through that first year without having my friend there to listen.

My auntie wrote us a letter which was a real comfort to both of us. One of the things she wrote was: 'There are so many clichés that people come out with at times of illness or death, and while you know many of them they are not what you want to hear right now. You must grieve in your own way, both individually and together, and whatever emotions you feel, from sadness to anger, it's okay. God understands. Even though Joshua had only a short life you must have precious memories which you will always treasure. Hang on to those.'

Direct speech we found so important. Often everyone is so exhausted, especially having to cope with another baby outside the hospital, that a lot of general conversation is lost in the moment. The words you remember clearly are those that are direct and clear, no messing, but with compassion. Time given to us was so important: we remember that we were not hurried along to make space for anything else. We could take our time, especially during the later stages towards death.

A very important thing was that someone recognized that we might want to take the opportunity of baptism for my son.

We love the fact that the chaplaincy have always kept in touch and that the annual memorial events have always taken place. Even if at times you are so consumed with grief, it's good to know you're not alone and these supports are there for you to call on and you're not forgotten.

I do also feel that contact from other mothers would have been of some comfort. Maybe this was offered during some of the post counselling – I can't remember. Sometimes things may not be an advantage at the time but may be more suitable a few months down the line. Continued care and support is important: your needs are different at different stages.

I found it helped to still talk about Deagan instead of keeping it all locked up inside. I have my moments where I stand in the shower or lie in the bath and have a good old cry. Sometimes I even still cry myself to sleep.

It would be useful, if there are any local bereavement groups around, that advertisements could be placed in very public places like shops, doctors' surgeries, community centres and leisure centres so that everyone can get to know about them. This includes any that might be run by any local churches.

When asked, 'How many children do you have?' I answer, 'I had two.' This is sometimes awkward, as people ask me what I mean. But I want to speak about Josie so she will not be forgotten.

Some of the ways that friends, family and community can support people who have been through this – offering to help, even just small things like offering a lift or doing some shopping. Be understanding when sometimes people just want to be left alone. Be a shoulder to cry on or just there to listen without feeling the need to cheer them up or change the subject.

When we were finally ready to, we sorted out our child's possessions and kept those that were most precious to us, but gave reminders to our wider family and friends who wanted something of theirs. What was left we gave to a charity shop that raised money for cancer; it helped to know that the funds raised would go towards his disease.

Other things include sponsoring things that connect with the child, holidays for those who cannot afford them, providing resources for children through organizations like Christian Aid or World Vision, donating their books to a school library, giving something in their memory to an organization they belonged to or sponsoring a special award or prize.

Insights from parents on what does not help

Medical staff we had known well for years suddenly backed off (as did friends and family outside the hospital) – the result was feeling that you had to manage other people's emotions as well as your own.

Someone speculating 'What sort of a life would he have had?'

Saying, 'I don't know how you carry on – if that happened to me I would kill myself.' This is hurtful. Does that mean you love your children more than I loved mine?

Saying, 'I lost my dog, granny, etc.' It's insulting to think it could be the same.

People avoiding us and not talking about our loss.

Birthdays, Christmas and anniversaries

The birthday of the lost child and Christmas can be the most painful times for a bereaved family. Here are some stories and reflections from some bereaved families on their experiences.

Birthdays – Kaitlyn loved her bubbles, so I suggested that friends and family blow some bubbles for Kaitlyn and take a photo to send to us.

I put these into a montage [easily created through sites such as <http://photobucket.com> and <www.flickr.com>] and it brought comfort and a smile to see the children blowing their bubbles for Kaitlyn. We also blew bubbles at her graveside and sent off balloons.

I set up a webpage on the Just Giving website [see Appendix 1] so that we and any other friends and family can put money on the webpage for Cameron's birthday, Christmas, Easter or at any time and put a message on there. It allows us to remember him as well as donating directly to charity (you can choose which charity you want to set up the webpage for). You are able to write about your child and put photos and video clips on the webpage.

Cameron's birthday is a few days after Christmas so that makes the whole Christmas period harder. However, we try to make his birthday as special as we can and have it as a day to focus on him. We go to the crematorium and take balloons and his birthday cards. We also organize a balloon release in our back garden for family and Cameron's friends (and we also do this on the anniversary of his death). We buy presents for Cameron's birthday too. The first year we named a star after him and we have a certificate that we were able to personalize – we wrote a poem on it for him.

When it comes to birthdays and Christmas, it can be quite tough. We take flowers to the cemetery and a balloon for Joshua's birthday. We light candles around the house.

When it is Jeremy and Nathan's birthdays we do birthday cards and flowers. We go to the hospital every May and it helps us to see the people who have supported us and been there for us when we needed them. They have done so much, we can't thank them enough.

When it is Josie's birthday we buy colourful candles and they are lit all day; we buy balloons and release them. We also do the balloons at Christmas. Our son got very upset when he had his fourteenth birthday as he was very aware that his sister never made it to this age.

Lauren loved dogs so we sponsored a guide dog for the blind for her third birthday, two months after she died. We also planted a cherry blossom tree in our garden which blossoms around her birthday. We still bring Lauren back a present from holiday, like a snow globe.

What we do is let the people who mattered to Tabea go up to the grave with us. We then sing 'Happy Birthday' or carols or whatever is appropriate for the occasion, then we decorate her 'garden' with the little gifts that everyone has brought with them, ensuring that all get involved who wish to.

For Kofi's birthday we always celebrate by going out for a meal where we used to take him and by visiting the National Memorial Arboretum to see his tree.

Supporting siblings

Most young people are resilient and can have unexpected strengths to survive a terrible loss. But they have their own distinctive needs:

- Siblings of a child who is ill or disabled can experience fear, worry, confusion, guilt, anger and embarrassment.
- Siblings need to be heard.
- They need to express their feelings, and above all else their desire to be involved in their sibling's care.
- Attention must be paid to them.
- Your other children need your help if they are to adapt to the family trauma and if you are to ease family tensions.

(Power and Orio, 2003, pp. 133–4)

Don't forget about siblings

No matter how young or old, they still matter and should not be kept in the dark. Tyrese was quite young, and still is, but we explained in very basic terms in a way which he would understand that Kofi was different from other babies. We explained to him that Kofi could get very poorly very quickly, and that Kofi one day would not be here. We explained that it was okay to be upset when it happens, but that Kofi would be okay and that when he went to heaven he would be going somewhere that would make him all better. Tyrese understood this in his own way – he said it would be like a 'sky hospital' where they would make him better. Tyrese still talks about Kofi most days, and we don't stop him.

It is important to acknowledge your surviving child's loss and support his or her grief cycle. We encouraged photographs and created a memory box together, and we communicate our feelings to one another; the good, the bad and the ugly are all acceptable. The statistics are high for a marriage break-up – in fact, 70 per cent of couples split after losing a child. It is so easy to lose touch with one another's feelings after your child's death. It takes respect, hard work and discipline to support one another and connect while enduring the pain of what life has dealt you.

Steve and Lesley Beard lost their daughter Stevie-Marie not long before her twelfth birthday. Stevie's brothers tend to bottle up their feelings.

Danny spends most of his time in his room. He doesn't like to talk about Stevie to his mum and dad, because he doesn't want to upset them. Occasionally he will let out all his feelings to his teaching assistant, Heather, though he will also talk to his brother Scott. Danny says that Stevie was not just his sister but his best friend. Because of his ADHD and conduct disorder, he feels that Stevie was the only one to understand him. He will love her and miss her for the rest of his life. The eldest brother, Ian, is particularly angry: his first daughter died when she was just four days old, and three years later he lost his sister. The double loss has made him very angry. Ian and Scott remain very proud that Stevie was their sister.

Stevie's sister Sheena, who wrote a poem about her sister and read it at the funeral, is still heartbroken and talks to Lesley a lot about her feelings. She is expecting a baby in June and intends to name the baby after Stevie. Sheena now runs a pub and Lesley now works there full time. This forces her to get out and talk to people. She values this, though it is hard work. Sheena's eldest daughter, Cheyenne, aged seven, used to play with Stevie a lot. Now she writes letters to her and draws pictures, which are taken to the grave. Cheyenne's younger sister, Lily, talks about Stevie a lot, especially about make-up and other girly things, but Lesley isn't sure whether it is her own memories or a rehearsing of things her sister's told her.

In engaging with the siblings it is important to appreciate their developmental level and talk to them in appropriate ways. They may appreciate creatively exploring issues through drawing or stories, for example. It is important that we don't underestimate their capacity to understand and engage with the issues and that we maintain a loving, trusting, open relationship. The Child Bereavement Charity and Winston's Wish both have resources for siblings that may be helpful (for details, see Appendix 1). The Paediatric Chaplaincy Network for GB&I (<www.bch.nhs.uk/departments/chaplaincy/paediatric_chaplaincy_network.htm>) and Red Balloon Learner Centres (<www.redballoonlearner.co.uk/media-centre/resources.htm>) have both sought to build partnerships with publishers and charities to produce resources that take seriously the issues and questions raised in the dying and death of a Christian child, and a series of publications is being developed.

Some of the most common grief reactions in children are anxiety, vivid memories, sleep difficulties, sadness and longing, anger and acting-out behaviour, guilt, self-reproach and shame, school problems and physical complaints (Dyregrov, 1991, pp. 14–15). I am not advocating that we should perceive ourselves as experts in diagnosing levels and types of appropriate grief, but we can learn not to make assumptions. Dyregrov raises a helpful point:

> Signs of this immediate, automatic emotional defence or protection mechanism may often be seen immediately after they get the message – many do not cry, some start to laugh, and many immediately start being very direct and practical, which is shown in such questions as: Can I use his bed now? Can I have his grey jacket? Can I take part in the funeral?
> (Dyregrov, 1991, p. 29)

Some of these questions can seem brash but we must take them in the context of the age and ability of the child.

Gender issues

This is not an area which has been very well researched and conclusions are mixed. However, it is clear that there is a danger of stereotyping. Parents may mention that boys more than girls don't talk about death and have difficulty showing feelings. This is clearly a generalization, but one which becomes more apparent as children reach adolescence. Boys have also been found to have more difficulty expressing their feelings in writing. Girls tend to have a good friend from whom they can get support, and also talk more at home about the death. Dyregrov attributes this to the way that boys and girls are socialized and play, where girls more commonly play in pairs and learn to express their feelings. Bereavement support is most often offered in ways that are more female-friendly, such as writing and talking (summarized from Dyregrov, 1991, pp. 52–4). These are points we may wish to bear in mind when we relate to siblings and children in church and the community.

Grandparents – double grief

Trevor Skeats, a psychology student on placement with BCH, has done some research on the role of grandparents in palliative and bereavement care, and what follows is a summary of what he found.

Irrespective of how well developed their own personal resources are, most parents rely to some extent on additional support from within their social structure in order to manage sudden and imminent family stress. Grandparents occupy a special place in family support networks, but the support they can offer can often be taken for granted. Yet that special place comes with a price attached: the price of mixed relationships and mixed emotions. The grandparents interviewed had a variety of partner relationships, including married, widowed and remarried after divorce. Those who had been widowed showed a sense of responsibility that this was a burden they alone had to bear, like the grandmother who took up residence beside the hospital 150 miles from her home just to be with her grandchild so that her son and daughter-in-law could meet their work commitments, or the grandfather who attended all his grandchild's hospital appointments whether or not the parent was able to attend. There was a sense of urgency to do something while they were still able to.

Relationships with former spouses who were also the natural grandparents needed special sensitivity if the grandchild's welfare was to be maintained. Even though this latter consideration was paramount, the personal grief and sense of impotence were present and added to the pressure.

If we are spiritual beings having a human experience, rather than the other way round, then grandparents and grandchildren are at each end of this experience and therefore closer to their spiritual being. This may account for what many grandparents regard as a special relationship. There was a sense that grandparents saw a need to encourage hope in their grandchild while trying desperately to maintain their own. Whether or not they were of a religious tradition, a spiritual belief made this encouragement easier to convey. The pain of losing a grandchild was exacerbated by the need to console their own child, who was now a grieving parent. Grieving for the dying grandchild can breed guilt for not tending to the pain of one's own child and supporting that child.

Feeling heard is perhaps all the grandparents need in order to allay their doubts, confusion and fears of being misunderstood. Having someone know that they really do care, not only for their sick grandchild but also for their grieving child, may well be comfort enough. With current patterns of church attendance, it may be that grandparents are our first or main point of contact with the family, and understanding their perspective can help us support them appropriately.

There may also be an added dimension to their grief, regarding the social factor of some grandparents being primary carers for their grandchildren. Perhaps some grandparents are in 'triple' grief.

A grandmother's story

Christmas for me is a time of joy and expectation, but 19 years ago it became a time of heartache and sorrow, My youngest son and his wife Sally were looking forward with excitement to the birth of their first baby. Sally had experienced a difficult pregnancy and on 27 December, the due date for the birth, she became unwell and was admitted to hospital into the delivery suite. A few hours later, with my son sitting at her bedside, without any warning Sally slipped into a coma and died. The hospital staff, unaware at the time that Sally was suffering from a serious illness, delivered my grandson by emergency caesarean section. A perfect baby boy, weighing in at eight pounds, Christopher – the name his parents had chosen for him – was a tiny ray of hope for my son and for Sally's and my families.

Within 48 hours it became apparent that Christopher had suffered brain damage from the timing of his birth, and then the final blow: we were told he had just a short time to live. I struggled with the look of disbelief on the face of my son, as all his hopes and dreams were taken from him in such a cruel way. Sally's parents cared for my son, taking him home with them as they were understandably struggling with their grief. My husband and I stayed at the hospital with Christopher, holding and loving him until he died on the evening of 30 December. I was so angry with God, asking 'Why these children?' for Sally at 22 was to me still a child.

I have come a long way since that Christmas so many years ago. I now have five grandchildren and have rejoiced in each one of their births, giving thanks to God, for they are all very precious, but Christopher will always hold a special place in my heart.

Separated parents

There are many issues around parents being separated in the care of a child. They could be divorced, separated, remarried, with another partner, estranged – and all these can cause issues when a child is dying. It needs to be established who has parental or guardian responsibility of the child so permission and consent can be agreed, and there are many other factors to take into account. There may not be a good relationship between the parents, though relationships may be good with the child. One parent may be perceived as being responsible for the child's condition. The guilt or resentment of absenteeism is something we frequently see, where the parent has not seen the child for a while, through choice or circumstances. This can lead to boundaries of legal responsibility being pushed when it comes to agreeing end-of-life rituals, funerals, etc. My recommendation is to clearly identify who has parental responsibility and seek to be a peacemaker or intermediary as needed.

Fundraising and campaigning

One of the frequent responses of a family losing a child is to fundraise on behalf of the child and to give to those organizations that provided help or support. The significance is not in the amount raised but in the action. Here are some examples:

We used the funeral money to buy a fully stocked bookcase for the children at BCH. Eighteen months later and we're still learning to adjust to life without our beautiful girl.

The best support we've received has been from Hope House, a children's hospice, who've never given up on us. We've started to raise some donations for the charity, albeit in a very small way, and are soon hoping to create and publish a website devoted to Willow.

We donated money on behalf of Deagan to the BCH Oncology Department and had a plaque made, which Dr English wrote and told me had been attached to some computer equipment that the money we donated had bought. It was a very good feeling to know that we may help in some way in the future.

Another way families express their loss is to campaign. This will inevitably be around the issue that affects or affected their child. Past examples have come from parents of children who have died as a result of gang, gun and knife crime. At the time of writing, 'Sarah's law' is a high-profile expression of this.

Campaigning is very helpful to our society because it is led by people who personally know how it feels, and this does have a credibility. They are motivated and won't let things drop. It also motivates local communities and national policies. Both fundraising and campaigning are therapeutic in several ways:

- Families feel they are doing something.
- Families can feel that something good can come out of their tragedy.
- Families feel able to give something back to the hospital, hospice, work of community nurses, etc.
- Gifts to hospitals, hospices, etc., can make life more pleasant for families who stay in the future.
- The name of the child may live on through being associated with the campaign or particular donation.

Organ donation

In a hospital there will be a member of staff responsible for organ donations and transplants (see Chapter 7), and it is this person's job to talk to a family about organ donation if it is an option. This is an emotive issue and one where we need to empower and facilitate rather than seek to persuade the family one way or another. If the family have taken this up, it can be of significant comfort that some good has come out of the death of their child.

A new normal

'A new normal' is a phrase that is being used to describe a family's realistic and healthy objective. I find this term very useful: it acknowledges that life will never be the same but that there is hope of a new way of living. It does not ignore their loss but gives permission for a new life, emphasizing that this is acceptable and doesn't dishonour their child. This is what we can help families work towards. But it must always be at the speed chosen by the family.

Whoever I was before, I am not that same person today.

(Louisa's mum, Sharon Moore)

Conclusion

The final thoughts for this chapter are summed up in a letter sent to a bereaved family:

> Dear Norm and Kay
>
> Sue and I were so saddened this morning when we learned that your precious daughter Donna had succumbed to her battle with leukaemia. Please know that we share in your pain and loss and deeply wish there was some way to lessen the anguish you must be going through. What a battle she fought during her brief five years of life. Donna always displayed courage despite the obvious pain she was in. Her memory and her life will be with us for ever.
>
> The loss of a child is an ache the heart was never meant to know. There is nothing I can say or do that will bring you consolation. But I do know that Donna could not have been loved more by any other parents. Your friends and relatives knew your sacrifices and your pain, which you tried hard not to let Donna see. All she knew was your unconditional love and affection, the soft touch of your hands, the warmth of your words. I know that your hearts are broken and that being with her when she died was most difficult. But I'm sure she was well aware that her loving parents were there with her during her last moments.
>
> Healing from the death of a child is most difficult and may take much time and patience. May thoughts of Donna and your love for each other sustain you and bring you comfort and strength. Take each day slowly. Cry with each other, talk to each other, hug each other. And try to remember that your friends and relatives are praying for you, weeping with you and sharing your sadness.
>
> We will call you next weekend to see what we can do for you. You will be in our thoughts and prayers.
>
> (Auz and Andrews, 2002, p. 125)

For reflection

- What are the strengths and weaknesses of your church, project or organization in its bereavement care pathway?
- How might your church or organization remember the birthday or anniversary of the death of a child with whom you had contact?
- How is fundraising helpful? Are there ways families can be supported in this activity?
- Are there ways you can use the experiences of those who have lost a child to help others in that position?
- Do you have people who can offer some of the long-term support that many families need?
- How are you supporting different members of the family? Who is being missed out? What can you do to address this?

6

Palliative care and bereavement in a hospital

In this chapter we hear from various professionals involved in the care of children in hospital, in order to help carers and those cared for better understand what to expect and what might be possible. The quality of care offered can make a significant difference, as these comments show:

My time in the Intensive Care Unit was helped along by a very special lady called Pauline. She was the most helpful lady I've ever met. She helped me arrange Kasey-Jayne's christening and all her blessings and she got me a room to stay in so I wasn't having to travel every day. She even came to her funeral, along with another nurse who treated Kasey-Jayne as her own.

The staff on PICU [the paediatric intensive care unit], especially, and every other member of the hospital staff that was involved in Deagan's care was absolutely brilliant and understanding. Every single thing was explained to us in terms we understood, which made a hard time that bit easier.

Perspectives from medical staff

Paediatric intensive care consultant – Fiona Reynolds

As a paediatric intensive care consultant, I co-ordinate the care of children admitted to the paediatric intensive care unit (PICU). In the UK around 12,000 children are admitted to PICU each year, and 1,200 of them come to the unit at BCH where I work. Most of the children who come to intensive care survive. The mortality rate is around 6–8 per cent, depending on the case mix of specialties the unit serves. The outcomes of many serious diseases have improved; however, each year around 90 children die in the unit where I work. The majority of children who die are born with a congenital disease or have chronic health problems throughout their life. Only a minority of children who die have been previously well children who are suddenly taken ill.

Children are admitted to PICU from a number of different routes. Children may be admitted after planned major surgery or because of the worsening of a condition which they have lived with for many years. Children may be admitted who were previously well but have suddenly contracted a life-threatening illness or been involved in a major accident. The family of a child may or may not have had some time to prepare themselves mentally for their child's admission to PICU. However, the nature of intensive care is to focus on achieving survival. Even when a child is admitted to PICU critically ill, our aim is to provide therapy aimed at survival.

The risk of death is discussed with families. Although the risk of death is accepted at an intellectual level the only way most families can function is to work on the assumption their child will survive. Preparation for death when a child is fighting for life and the family are still helping the child battle for life is something that cannot be done.

Some children die in PICU during active resuscitation; the child's heart stops and there is nothing that can be done to restart it. In this situation families may or may not have some warning of the possibility of the heart stopping. Other children who die in PICU may be kept alive but in a situation where there is no hope of recovery. Modern medicine may be able to keep the child alive for another day, week or month but bring no hope of life outside of PICU. In this situation I advise families that the intensive care should be withdrawn as it is futile and will not lead to recovery.

Most children who die in PICU are so sick and dependent on machines that they have to be kept sedated to allow the tubes and machines to stay in place. As a result, most children who die are not aware that they are dying and cannot be woken to be made aware of their imminent death.

Families of children dying in PICU are offered the opportunity to talk to a number of different people. They can talk to the family liaison nurses, who have specific training in talking to families in this situation and who can offer practical help such as car park passes or accommodation advice. My role is to ensure the family understand the medical issues surrounding the child's diagnosis, treatment and prognosis. If the child is dying, the family need to understand what medical therapy has been given to the child and why it is not working. Chaplaincy staff are available 24/7 if requested.

Usually I speak with the parents or guardians on their own. I offer to speak with anyone they want present, but most parents wish to hear news themselves before sharing it with the wider family. I usually ask if they need me to talk to anyone in the family, and at this point some will ask me to break the news. Some parents find it particularly difficult to break the news to the siblings of the dying child. They often ask me what they should say. I tell them to keep it very simple but to ensure the siblings know that it is not their fault that the child is dying, as children can sometimes believe death is a punishment for something they have done wrong. I also say they should explain that the illness which affects the dying child does not affect anyone else in the family (if this is true), as children may worry that others in the family may also die. I say that the parents should say they are upset, but that it is okay to be upset as it is very sad when someone you love dies.

When a child is dying in PICU and can be sustained for some time but without hope of recovery, the medical advice is to withdraw intensive therapy and switch to palliative therapy. The family may believe the medical opinion is wrong and ask for a second opinion, or they may agree with the assessment of the medical staff that the child is going to die but cannot bear to accept the death at that particular time. In either situation, it is important to allow the family time and give them information in a way and at a pace they can handle if the family and medical staff are going to be able to work together for the child. When a child is dying it is important that the family think about who they want present at the bedside. They should also think about the atmosphere they want to create around the child. Prompting families to think about what atmosphere the child would want can result in the situation becoming more personalized and focused on the individual child's preferences.

Some families need more time than others to accept the death of a child. In PICU this may mean supporting the life of a dying child for a number of days while the family comes to terms with the child's imminent death. Details on the process of dying are important, to allow a family to prepare themselves for what happens during the process of death. If the child is likely to have laboured breathing and turn blue at the end of life it is important that this is explained to the family. We explain the child will go to the mortuary and that his or her colour will change; the mortuary is cold, and the child's skin will feel cold to the touch.

Macmillan paediatric nurse/oncology outreach nurse – Nicki Fitzmaurice

The purpose of my role is to support children and young people (CYP), their families and those professionals who care for them after they have had a cancer or leukaemia diagnosis. Support will sometimes last until long after the CYP have finished treatment and are cured; sadly, for others support will continue until they eventually die. I will continue to make contact with bereaved families for up to two years after their child's death. I work as a part of a multidisciplinary team that also includes social workers, doctors, play specialists and psychologists.

During the course of their cancer treatment I will make contact with CYP and their families, offering practical advice and someone they can talk to who understands about the drugs they will be receiving, the types of problems they might encounter and ways they can help themselves. I will see CYP and their families in hospital and in their homes. I will also visit their nursery, school or college to speak to the teachers about how to continue education during treatment. In order to keep CYP at home or as close to home as possible, I talk to, teach practical skills to and visit local healthcare community teams and hospitals that help care for them. Having known the CYP during their cancer treatment can make the difficult job of supporting both them and their families through palliative care a little easier. I will have met and visited the CYP and family previously and hopefully established a rapport with both them and their local community team. Sometimes CYP and their families can be given the news that they are now incurable and continue to live for many months, perhaps years with their disease. For others their disease progresses quickly and their death happens within a matter of months. It is always their doctor who gives the news that the disease is no longer curable. The news may be given to just the family or to the CYP and the family; the age of the CYP and individual wishes of the family will guide this decision. I am usually present at this meeting. I work as part of a Macmillan team that offers 24-hour on-call support for CYP reaching the end of their lives, and am trained to be able to assess symptoms and suggest strategies and drugs that may make a difference. I will continue to visit the CYP and families during this time to offer support.

Families often struggle with the notion of letting their child know that his or her life is coming to an end, primarily because of a need to protect their child as much as they can. My role is to discuss with families their fears and the potential benefits that open communication can offer. It is not my role to 'force the issue'; I will, however, tell families that if CYP ask questions exploring whether they are dying, I will answer sensitively but honestly. Experience has taught me that many CYP are aware they are dying and value the opportunity to plan their future and talk openly about their hopes and fears, however short the time span might be.

My key learning over the many years I have practised in this role is concerned with developing my ability to listen attentively and control my need to try and 'fix' things. As a symptom control specialist, I find it much easier in discussions with CYP and families to focus in on, for example, the issue of pain. This is my territory, and the simplest strategy for me is to steer conversations towards physical symptoms and medical issues; this makes the conversation my agenda and in an area where I feel in control. This may not, however, be a conversation that is important to the CYP or family. My learning has come from allowing them rather than me to lead conversations and staying with their agenda. For those of you reading this, the idea of allowing CYP and families the space to discuss their agenda might seem an obvious outcome of any conversation. However, for those of us used to 'focusing and fixing' healthcare-related problems, it can be difficult to listen to concerns behind those we are comfortable with and accept that there may be nothing more therapeutic than listening.

I continue to be amazed at the ability of brothers and sisters to support their dying brother or sister. In my experience, to do this most effectively siblings need to be aware of the situation. Again, this can be difficult for parents to accept, wanting to protect their children, especially younger ones. Brothers and sisters invariably want to be included and cope better with bereavement if they have been part of decisions and caregiving. A brother, aged 12 and sister aged 11 were invited by their parents to discuss whether it would be better to bury or cremate their brother, aged seven, who was in the last weeks of his life. I was invited to be a part of this conversation, which took place in their home. The brother and sister spent some time asking about the process of burial and cremation and what it entailed. Their final conclusion was that they chose to bury their brother in the local church graveyard. The brother and sister rejected the idea of cremation because they felt that their brother's ashes would be returned to them with the cancer's ashes too. If they buried him, his body would eventually disappear and they would have their brother's bones without the cancer. Several years later I met the brother and sister and highlighted the conversation I had been privileged to be a part of. Each of them commented on how valuable it had been to have been active family members in conversations about their brother's death. Knowing he was going to die also allowed them the choice to spend time with him, something they would not have thought to do if they had been under the impression he would live.

Clinical nurse specialist in donor care – Rachel Hodge

The number of children who would benefit from transplantation far exceeds the number of donor organs and tissues available for transplant. Although the UK population is supportive of transplantation, donation rates remain among the lowest in Europe. End-of-life decisions remain with the living long after the death of a loved one and have been implicated in abnormal and complicated grief. As families have a limited opportunity to consider donation, it is imperative that the approach and discussion about donation is carried out by a specifically trained, knowledgeable, family-focused, motivated healthcare professional who will have time to discuss all aspects of the donation decision-making process.

The clinical nurse specialist (CNS) in donor care working within the hospital is able to offer support to families who wish to discuss the options of donating organs and tissues for transplantation after the death of their child. Timely involvement of the CNS by the team caring for a dying child means there can be appropriate facilitation of planned and collaborative discussions with families which can allow for greater information-sharing. This collaborative approach enables families to make an informed decision as the CNS is able to give the most up-to-date information to the family and assist them in their questions. Many families find the donation of organs and tissues for transplantation a positive experience and a source of great comfort during a distressing time. All families where there is a possibility for donation should be given the option of donation; by not doing this we are depriving them of the opportunity to feel this positivity and comfort. More detailed information about what organs and tissues can be donated for transplantation as well as stories told by families who have donated organs and tissues and have found a great deal of positivity in making this gift can be found at <www.uktransplant.co.uk>.

Perspectives from non-medical staff

Senior chaplain, Great Ormond Street – Jim Linthicum

Confusion, questioning and uncertainty in a variety of forms tend to be some of the cornerstones of the dying, death and bereavement processes for all who are involved – whether they are the one who is dying, the family or the staff. In some situations a variety of 'experts' are called – including key members of the psycho-social team such as psychologists, social workers, bereavement or end-of-life care staff and sometimes even ethicists. While in the old days chaplaincy had a distinctive role to play in its religious guise, nowadays role diffusion can be a risk. What then are some of the ways in which these spiritual caregivers can be understood to have a distinctive role?

They can be mediators of hope. One of the key concerns surrounding death is the nature of the future. That future affects everyone involved in many different ways. Some parents worry about 'where their child will go'. They also wonder how they are going to get through the whole situation themselves or, indeed, if they will. The future for these people can seem truly hopeless. However, they often turn to the spiritual caregivers to find any strands of hope that might be available. This can include guidance about the afterlife; resources for the future for the bereaved; and ways, often through ritual, to transform pain into potential. Spiritual caregivers can also be those with whom the dying and bereaved can search for meaning. The resources of the spiritual caregiver which go beyond the material, static and 'earthbound' sometimes free up new possibilities of ways of looking at situations. Once again, child bereavement will probably always lack full meaning, particularly for those looking from the outside in, but some families and children want so badly to bring meaning out of mystery that having a resource for exploration can be invaluable. One method for finding this meaning, and indeed hope, is to employ transcendence, which in this case means developing the long view. In this particular area spiritual caregivers are not totally distinctive from other practitioners. However, they can call upon resources which others may find uncomfortable or outside of their remit.

Hospital Play Service – Helen Costello

Support provided by the specialist Play Service generally begins at the diagnostic stage of the family's journey and continues throughout their medical treatment. Our primary role within the Trust is to provide emotional support for children and young people of all ages and their families. Play is used to provide education regarding condition and treatment, as a distraction tool for procedures and in a therapeutic sense to allow for safe release of feelings and aid normality. Our support is provided depending on the individual needs of the child and family and takes into account their wishes and beliefs. Our involvement with the family involves providing resources such as books and information that will enable the family to inform the child, and siblings, about palliative care and bereavement. Emotional support will continue to be provided to both the patient and the siblings throughout this process.

One of the primary roles of the hospital play specialist is to act as an advocate for the child. This continues during this period where the wishes of the child are taken into account and respected. It may include decisions about where the child continues palliative care treatment or wishes for his or her funeral. Therapeutic play continues to be provided to allow for the safe release of feelings, and we will encourage all of the family to take part, providing some normality, and encourage family time. Support continues to encourage the patient to comply with palliative treatment. This may include using incentive charts and rewards. For children and young people experiencing palliative care, many of them will have had thoughts about whom they would like precious things to be left to. Many of them will also like to leave happy memories behind. This may be a memory box, sand bottles or anything they wish. The hospital play specialist can provide the resources, encouragement and emotional support to achieve this. Our experience suggests that it can be helpful to provide normality up to the point of death, that the word 'death' should not be seen as unmentionable and that families can feel a connection with the hospital and staff for many years.

Hospital-based youth worker – Charlotte Frith

I work on a referral basis with young people, including self-referrals. The majority of my time is spent supporting young people on a one-to-one basis who need emotional support with issues, and where possible enabling them to re-engage with their community. I get involved with young people when a referral is received by the adolescent support service. This could be because the young person is struggling with something such as being in hospital, being away from family and friends or being in isolation. I work with young people with many different conditions, including diabetes, liver conditions, cancer, cystic fibrosis, sickle cell anaemia, and young people with multiple medical conditions. I offer support to the young person by talking through issues with him or her, providing normalizing activities (I am often seen as 'playing') and discussing the usual issues young people have to deal with, from friends, self-esteem and risk-taking behaviour to life and death issues.

I don't normally get a referral because a young person is dying; however, if I am already working with him or her my involvement continues. I sometimes receive referrals for siblings whose brother or sister is dying – it's a very hard time for the family and the siblings need space to talk freely. I explain to parents that I am someone for the young people to talk to, outside of the medical team, someone who they can share their worries with without worrying about how it will affect me (they are often concerned about how their parents will worry if they tell them how they are feeling). At times this support can be providing a safe space for young people to explore emotions and issues that they don't feel they can raise anywhere else.

Mortuary technician – Sarah Davis

The purpose of my role is to manage the day-to-day activities within the mortuary. This includes receiving children, preparing for family visits, preparing and assisting at postmortems, releasing children to the families who may want to take their dead child home or to funeral directors, and educating staff on mortuary procedures. I try and offer support to everyone I come in contact with. I know that the death of a child not only has a traumatic effect on the family but impacts in different ways on every healthcare professional who has known the child and the family. No one wants to say the word 'mortuary', let alone have to contact mortuary staff, which makes it more important to show families, hospital staff, funeral directors and police that we are here and will try and help them as much as we can through this time.

Support can be shown in different ways. One way, I feel, is to show that the children in my mortuary are treated with respect and dignity. People associate mortuaries with elderly people dying but the thought of children dying is very upsetting. I find that families and staff are concerned over how the child is treated. When I have any calls about the children I am dealing with I always refer to the children by their Christian names; this helps in getting information across to families and staff.

The environment where a family comes to see their child is very important. I feel that with the right decoration, furniture and facilities this can show families and staff that the hospital is still caring for the deceased child. I assist staff in placing the children in our Rainbow Suite. This area has a bedroom, sitting room, toilet and a garden. A family may make as many visits as they wish. I encourage staff to visit this area to familiarize themselves with the facilities on offer. I talk through the practical aspects of how to gain entry into the suite, moving the child and making the child presentable for the family. I feel this helps the staff as they are able to prepare a family for what the rooms look like and how their child is going to be placed. Also I am letting staff know I am available if they need any help.

The most difficult topic for staff to discuss is that of postmortems. I show staff what the postmortem room looks like, what is involved in a postmortem and what information on why a child has died can be gained for the family. Most importantly I try to show staff that the child and the family are our top priority. My profession can be difficult at times but very rewarding.

Bereavement counsellor and psychotherapist – Mary Glover

I am an experienced independent psychotherapist working with bereaved children, adolescents and adults, I also work as bereavement counsellor at BCH. My role is to provide therapy to clients, working within the relevant professional codes of ethics. Individuals in need of therapy may have access to hospital counsellors, psychotherapists and psychologists but referral criteria vary. At BCH I am available at any time after the child has died to staff, siblings and primary carers of the child. I would only be involved if there is a specific psychological need, but this cannot be predicted by the type of death as several factors that contribute to family and individual resilience are multifactorial. I offer psychological interventions based on an assessment of needs. Where appropriate and with permission I encourage engagement with the local community, e.g. GP, health visitor or faith community.

In the long term the psychological process of grieving involves making sense of what has happened, locating the deceased child in the present and establishing ongoing relationships that include memories of the child. It is often important to engage in ritual. As a pastoral helper you will need to listen to the story, which will be told and retold, and to validate the grieving person's experience. Often people need to be reassured that they are 'not going crazy', and that they do need time to make sense of their story, including expressing their very raw feelings. Grief will highlight existing family or individual difficulties, especially where attachment has been a problem. The key message that cannot be overemphasized is: if you have concerns, make a referral – to the client's GP if no other service is available. Being aware of your own skill level is vital. Remember: if someone tells you that you are the only person that can help them – it's never true. Manage your own time: giving a bereaved person a specific time [with a specified ending] is therapeutically the kindest gift you can offer. If you are referring people on to specialist help the British Association for Counselling and Psychotherapy (BACP) as well as the United Kingdom Council for Psychotherapy (UKCP) will be able supply the names of therapists in private practice for clients able to pay [further information from <www.bacp.co.uk> and <www.psychotherapy.org.uk>]. Making a referral to voluntary agencies can be fraught with difficulties, although those who hold the status of being a BACP-recognized organization will be able to offer appropriate support. Other organizations may not be able to offer a similar level of service, but will be able to give you a list of their counsellors who hold BACP-accredited status.

Conclusion

When supporting a family whose child is in hospital, it can be helpful to be aware of the different types of support that may be available and to encourage the family to ask about what resources may be available for them.

For reflection

- Did anything in this chapter surprise you or make you more aware of the range of resources available to children and families when their child is in hospital?

- Do you have a database of chaplains in local hospitals so you can make a swift referral if a family you know have a child in hospital?
- Do you have congregation members who may be interested in volunteering at a local hospital or hospice? There are a lot of opportunities, and knowledge and experience gained can be helpful to both the individual and the church.
- How can you support members of your church who work in the caring professions?

7

Palliative care and bereavement in the community

This chapter offers perspectives from specialists in the community and again is designed to inform carers and families about some of the forms of help available to them and their children.

Parish priest – Duncan Hill-Brown

Chloe was born with a complex collection of life-limiting and ultimately terminal disabilities which meant that she would die young. Ensuring her life was as full as possible was a priority for her parents. Arriving on the scene as the new vicar in the weeks leading up to Chloe's death was significant. I met Chloe and her family several times during the first couple of weeks – at church services and at school. Then, suddenly, on my second Sunday the local GP (also a church member) telephoned to tell me that Chloe had been rushed into hospital, having stopped breathing. What followed was an intense three days spent with the family at the hospital. When I arrived in ITU Chloe's mother turned to me and said, 'Good, you are here. It's all right now. I prayed that nothing would happen to Chloe until our new vicar arrived. You are here so it will be okay.' This was humbling but also overwhelming. What followed was basically a vigil, rather like a Gethsemane experience. We watched and waited, we celebrated and remembered. We talked through the pain Chloe had already experienced in her life. They told stories. We laughed and cried. We sat in silence. There was only one chair so we took turns to sit in it.

I spent time with Helen's parents and the boys. Helen's parents were bringing the boys in, but they had to spend a lot of time outside ITU. My role with the boys in particular was to help them to understand that Chloe was dying. We played lots of games in the corridors and the family room. They didn't have many questions. They had learnt to take life one day at a time.

There was real dignity surrounding Chloe's death. The medical team were constantly monitoring her for signs of brain stem activity. After the life support was switched off (I was there with Dave and Helen), Chloe began to breathe on her own. It only lasted a few hours, but it did mean that Chloe died in her mother's arms. When it became clear that the end was near, the boys came in and the hearts and forget-me-nots that BCH use in such situations were used. At the end of the afternoon we all went outside and the boys let off two pink helium balloons. Then I phoned school and told them that Chloe had died.

It is a rare privilege to be able to do the funeral of someone you have accompanied in death; to do so for a child was even more of a privilege. Chloe's school was closed for the funeral and the church was packed with six- and seven-year-olds, their parents and staff. It was her world that gathered to celebrate her life and remember her. The songs were ones sung at school. Her favourite story was read. Pink balloons were let off at the end of the service. Her coffin was placed out of direct view at the request of Helen and Dave because of their concern that other children might be upset by seeing it. Chloe's funeral is still talked about.

My reflections as a parish priest are that it is important to see the big picture. Working within the community gives a unique perspective. Working with the family, school and wider community requires one to hold in tension the concerns, views and pain of all involved. The parish priest – or anyone wearing a dog-collar – is often seen as God's representative in the situation. If you are invited in by the family, there is an important, quite possibly unspoken implication of a recognition of God's presence with the family. Seek to offer empathy rather than sympathy. Allow yourself to be vulnerable – a genuine response of 'weeping with those who weep'. Don't lose sight of your own faith experience when surrounded by the grief and suffering of others – maintain your faith perspective. Be prepared for an ongoing journey and an element of 'bonding and entangling' that can go on for years in a parish context. Work collaboratively and draw on the wisdom and experience of others in a multidisciplinary approach where possible (e.g. GP, schools, chaplaincy team at the hospital and medical staff).

Senior general practitioner – Colin Eagle

Words will always be inadequate to support parents awaiting the imminent death of a loved child, or to comfort parents who have been bereaved, but words allied to practical support and empathy can greatly help parents, and the general practitioner (GP) is in a unique position to offer this.

The GP may have been the first health professional to be alerted to serious illness in the child, and may have referred the child to specialists. The behaviour of the GP at this initial stage is crucial. A good GP must be able to listen to parental concerns and be alert to the often subtle and discreet signs of the early stages of serious childhood illness. He or she must respond and act on parental concern even if there is no initial clear evidence of disease. Experienced doctors often freely state that if the parents are concerned that a child is ill then the child is, until proved otherwise. The sensitivity, kindness, understanding and helpfulness of the doctor at this early stage is of paramount importance.

Primary care is available every week of the year and the GP may continue to be the main initial source of ongoing healthcare for the child and parents. The GP may need to explain more about the child's disease, as parents may not have fully understood or comprehended what the specialists have told them. He or she will need to continue to listen to the parents' worries and concerns that their beloved child may suffer pain or distress, and respond with appropriate reassurance of the ability of modern medicine to relieve such distress. The GP must allow for the parents to show anger, grief and overt emotion, which may sometimes be directed towards healthcare professionals and perhaps to the GP. Such displays of emotion can be very difficult for the GP to cope with during a busy surgery or after a long demanding day, and the GP must be aware of the emotion caused within him- or herself at the suffering of one young patient and associated family. Caring for a child with terminal illness can be very emotionally demanding, requiring a difficult professional detachment, which is necessary for the doctor to maintain his or her mental health but which must not be communicated to the parents as detachment but as professional concern, empathy and caring. Allied to this support is the continuing need for clinical skill and judgement in managing the child's ongoing healthcare needs.

Soon after bereavement the role of the GP is vital in helping the parents, through sympathy and understanding, the temporary prescription of a medication if necessary and through appropriate sickness absence from work certification. Bereaved parents will invariably have feelings of guilt, feeling that they could have cared better for their lost child, that the outcome could have been different if they had taken the child to the doctor sooner or if they had acted differently. Such feelings of guilt are normal and the parents must be informed of this; the GP must allow for expressions of emotion, anger and of the seeming unfairness of life. Counselling may be helpful to the parents, but referral should only be made when the parents feel they wish it and when they feel it will help them. The GP should be aware that the bereavement process may take years before the parents can feel able to function normally again, and the GP must never imply that the parents will 'get over it' or that after a few months of bereavement they should be 'back to normal'. The GP should be aware of the 'conspiracy of silence' that bereaved parents often find so hurtful – that people and family try not to talk about their loss and dead child for fear of upsetting the parents, when in fact the parents wish to talk about their child and it is the seeming denial of the child's existence that they find so upsetting.

Parents may feel they cannot cope after the loss of their child, but it is okay for the GP to sensitively let them know that they will cope because they have no other choice, particularly if the parents have other children to care for. Getting back to work and normal living can be therapeutic for the parents, and the GP should facilitate this at the appropriate time. The GP needs to be alert to the onset of depression in either bereaved parent and in siblings, and to arrange for appropriate assessment and treatment. The GP can greatly ease the burden of child death and bereavement if he or she practises in this way.

Coroner

All deaths need to be registered, and before you can register a death you need either a medical certificate giving the cause of death, issued by a doctor, or a certificate issued by the Coroner after he or she has investigated the death. Coroners are independent judicial officers who work with a team. The Coroner is appointed by the local council but is accountable to the High Court. Deaths are reported to the Coroner and an inquest may be held when a person:

- has died a violent or unnatural death;
- has died a sudden death of which the cause is unknown;
- has died during an operation or within 24 hours of an operation;
- is on the 'at risk' register, or part of a family where another child is or was on the 'at risk' register, or is being privately fostered;
- has died in prison or in any other circumstances required by law.

In the case of a sudden or suspicious death the Coroner does not need permission to do a postmortem, but normally families will be asked to sign a form confirming they have been informed of what samples have been taken and how they will be disposed of. Anyone can report a death to a Coroner but most are reported by doctors or, in some circumstances, the police.

There are two main types of inquest. The first is fast-track with no postmortem, where the facts are straightforward; this is usually completed within a few days of death and the Coroner issues documents to allow the funeral to take place. In more complex cases, such as a road traffic accident or non-accidental or suspicious deaths, there will be a longer inquest, often with a postmortem. Sometimes the inquest is opened and adjourned and the body released to the family with an interim certificate to allow the funeral to take place, but investigations continue. There will then be a hearing once all the facts are gathered and the cause of death is determined by the Coroner. Families and the public are normally able to attend inquests which are held at the Coroner's Court and travelling expenses may be reimbursed to families. Further details may be found at <www.tcf.org.uk/leaflets/leinquests.html>.

Funeral director Thomas Bragg and Sons

The main role of the funeral director is to provide sufficient information on available options and to arrange for the final choices to be carried out in the best possible manner. The funeral of a child is one of the more difficult things that funeral directors have to deal with. Most funeral directors should be able to advise what facilities are available in their local area, and be able to find information from other sources, if appropriate. They will also indicate the associated costs of different options – while most authorities are sensitive in relation to charges for children's funerals these are still payable and should be established in advance. To the best of my knowledge most funeral directors carry out straightforward children's funerals on a 'cost only' basis, or often less.

The first decision is whether to have a cremation or burial. When this decision has been made the funeral director can provide choices and contacts for the family – religious or non-religious, local contacts for churches or organizations of all denominations and beliefs – and suggest places where a ceremony might be held. The choices made by the family are many and varied and can range from a full cortège, church service and committal to a quiet and private graveside remembrance. The funeral director must provide sufficient information to allow the family to come to a decision, and must then support them in fulfilling their wishes.

The presentation of the child is very important, irrespective of whether the parents wish to view or spend any time in the chapel of rest, as their last impression, real or imagined, will remain with them for a long time. To this end we suggest that favourite, personal clothing be provided, along with special possessions, for the time leading up to the funeral. Viewing the deceased is a very personal matter, and reactions vary. The choice of a suitable coffin, casket or crib-style basket can be of great importance in the process of remembrance and in feeling that the 'correct' thing has been done, and funeral directors can advise on the wide variety available.

How the day is organized can greatly help the bereaved cope. It is important that the occasion proceeds as planned by the family and that nothing unexpected occurs to cause any additional distress or concern.

The outline of the day is usually discussed at an early stage so timings can be established and an initial framework prepared. We need to allow for travel arrangements for mourners, the attendance of the required officiant, transport arrangements for the coffin and the family, the estimated time and content for the ceremony and suitable arrangements made for the family afterwards. We try to interpret the wishes of the family in all cases, and aim to provide advice, support and unobtrusive practical assistance.

Senior crematorium technician – Paul Rayner

Families are far more involved in the preparation and choices around their child's funeral now than a generation ago; there is now a strong sense of 'this is a life to be honoured', however brief that life may have been. More families are opting for a burial rather than a cremation as this gives a sense of permanence in the place of remembering. This choice is one a family may wish to discuss with the minister. Many public cemeteries now have a children's section and this may be true of some churchyards as well. The fees for a burial will vary depending on the local authority. In Solihull the fee for the grave and interment for a person under 16 is £350, plus £141 if the chapel is used. Some families will opt to have a service in church first. If the family opt for cremation, in Solihull the fee for a child under two years of age is £40 and £88 up to 16 (2010 prices). Particularly if the service is a cremation, thought needs to be given to the length of the service before the booking is finalized. A short, simple, family-only service may fit easily into the normal crematorium time span, but a fuller service with a number of tributes may well require a longer chapel time and normally this needs to be booked at the outset. Families should ask the funeral director early on what format of music is used at the crematorium so that appropriate arrangements can be made if there are special songs to be played.

The end of the service can be a particularly difficult time. At a burial there is not usually a hurry, but with a cremation there may be another service following on soon afterwards. If the family have asked for the curtains to be left open they may want to spend some time at the coffin, saying farewell. Particular sensitivity is required from funeral directors and clergy in judging when to start persuading the family to move away.

If a family chooses cremation there are usually a considerable number of options for the disposal of the ashes which need to be discussed with the family, and whether or not they want some form of memorial or plaque. If the child is buried, what sort of headstone is wanted? Funeral directors will be able to advise, as public cemeteries and churchyards will have regulations that families need to know about before a design for a memorial is finalized.

Staff nurse in a children's hospice – Rob Bresnen

I work as part of a team of professionals, including care assistants, physiotherapists, community workers, general practitioners and a paediatrician. The hospice is a charity – there is no charge to the families of children we look after. We accept referrals from anyone involved in the child's care, including family members. All referrals are considered by a panel of nurses and doctors to determine whether they meet our criteria before being accepted. Sometimes a referral is urgent, where the child is not expected to live very long, often following accidents, critical illness or sudden deterioration in long-standing medical conditions. In these cases we respond as quickly as we can, often arranging the transfer from hospital within a few hours, but usually we have more time to plan ahead. Parents and children will have an opportunity to visit the hospice beforehand and decide for themselves what care we can offer them.

We offer respite care to children with life-limited conditions, so that their families can have a break. This is often the only chance the families of these seriously ill children get to have a break from the daily routine of caring for their child. This allows parents precious time together, and with their other children. As the child approaches the end of life the nurses at the hospice, working closely with a paediatric palliative care consultant, can offer highly specialized care to help manage the child's symptoms, such as pain, nausea or fitting.

When Jack and Marie arrived with their child I welcomed them to the hospice, and showed them to our Family Care Suite, which has a family bedroom, with a double bed, attached to the child's bedroom. I worked hard to reassure them, and to find out what they wanted from the hospice. It became apparent that they wanted to be in control, to make all the decisions on their son's future. For three months he had been a patient in a hospital – now they wanted him to be their baby. I assured them that we respected their wishes, and by the end of the first night in the hospice Mum had told her husband that she was happy at the hospice and didn't want to go home with her baby. They remained at the hospice for the next three weeks. During that time Mum carried out most of the care. We advised them on the best medication to use to control his symptoms and on feeding, as well as providing emotional support for his family and helping to prepare them for their son's death. When he eventually passed away it was peacefully, in his sleep, in his mother's arms, with his dad and grandma close by. It was simple, quiet and dignified, just as his parents had wanted.

School counsellor – Bev Palmer

I had been working as a youth counsellor in a secondary school when I was asked to support the school leadership team, who were trying to cope with the hysteria that had come from the sudden death of a popular year 11 girl from meningitis. Grief is a messy process that does not present itself in any ordered and predictable fashion. Validating the young people's feelings and experience does rely on those in authority to acknowledge and embrace the moment. Forcing the young people to carry on with the day in the normal structured way pushes the grief inwards, and the risks of transference, projection and aggressive outbursts are heightened. Schools are often best equipped to cope if they have someone on site who is trained and qualified and aware of all of the above, as he or she can often be on hand to help support teaching staff to cope with their own grief as well as their strategic management of the situation. For schools not fortunate enough to have their own counsellor the local education authority should provide support where necessary.

The advantage for me and the school in this situation was that I knew the young people and staff and was able to act very quickly, providing systems and strategies to help them cope.

Support for young people includes:

- providing a quiet retreat for the close friends to meet together;
- offering one-to-one and group support for close friends;
- setting up a memory board where the young people can place poems or pictures;
- having a condolence book in a public place for all to read or write in;
- having year-group assemblies supported by key staff to talk about the grief process and advising tutors to watch out for signs in young people of not coping;
- sending a letter home to parents to alert them to the situation and their young people's grief, and the support in place;
- preparing the young people for the funeral and planning their participation;
- having the local chaplains on call for further support;
- facilitating peer support.

Support for staff includes:

- offering debrief sessions at the start and end of each day;
- providing leaflets and literature to read that explain the grief process;
- having drop-in sessions for staff to come and talk about their own grief or concerns;
- facilitating peer support.

It is important to note that young people cope best if facilitated and guided through the tasks of grief. They will and do take ownership of creative tributes that give them a cathartic expression of their love and depth of care as well as despair for the friend they have lost and those that remain behind. This is often the first time that young people have had to cope with death at such close quarters; it can be very scary for them and can trigger all manner of deeper anxieties. But left to talk among themselves, with caring adults and professionals aiding them, they will come through their 'dark night of the soul'. Nothing will ever be the same again for them, but they will have a new language and understanding of our human condition and a healthy regard for the process of grief as well as the tasks of grief.

A memorial was held and planned by the young people at the school for those not able to attend the funeral. It was a moving tribute and celebration of a life short-lived. From the PowerPoint presentation of personal photographs and fitting music to the precious words of prose and the setting off of 100 balloons with messages attached, there was not a dry eye in the place, but from this came a deep and mutual respect and a building of a stronger community within the school.

How primary schools can help

This advice is relevant for both siblings and friends of a child who has died:

- Be familiar with children's home background, including faith and culture, and talk about religious and cultural beliefs with them.
- Allow children to express their grief.
- Allow children time to fully understand and come to terms with what has happened;
- Encourage children to ask questions, and be consistent in the answers you give.
- Accept children's responses to what has happened – children are not a homogenous group.
- Involve children in ceremonies and rituals where possible.
- Explain the range of emotional responses associated with bereavement.
- Encourage young children to engage in play.
- Help children's peer group to understand what has happened.
- Help children to organize their memories of the person who has died.

Children may need specialized professional support because of complicated grief if, several months after the death, they:

- appear sad or depressed all the time;
- are not able to relax or have not returned to activities which they enjoyed before bereavement;

- lack self-esteem or express feelings of worthlessness;
- become persistently aggressive;
- seem withdrawn;
- are suffering from bouts of physical illness;
- are consistently tired;
- have lost weight and are not regaining it;
- become involved in out-of-character behaviour such as stealing or lying;
- pretend that nothing has happened. (From Brown, 2009)

Complementary therapist – Pankaj Shah

Some people find complementary therapies helpful in palliative care and bereavement. Both the child and the parent can benefit from complementary therapies to help with physical, emotional and psychological symptoms. The therapies can help with symptoms related to the child's illness as well as side effects of treatments being received. They can also help with the person's spiritual well-being. Where the child's condition causes multiple disabilities, many of the complementary therapies can enhance the child's sensory experience through touch and/or smell as well as through the use of music and lighting during the therapy session. During times of stress and anxiety, complementary therapies can promote a sense of peace, calmness and relaxation. Through the benefits of complementary therapies, parents also gain a sense of feeling able to cope with the situation they are in. Furthermore, after the child dies, complementary therapies can support the parents through bereavement.

Many therapists can teach family members simple therapy techniques that the family members can utilize at home for the benefit of the child and other family members. This is particularly valuable as it can promote quality time and interaction between the parent and child; it promotes bonding; and it gives the child an opportunity to talk about his or her thoughts and feelings with the parent. Often, parents feel disempowered in being able to support their child with complex and palliative health problems. Learning some simple complementary therapy skills gives them back a sense of being able to help and support their child in a positive way. Also it can bring the whole family together, as different family members can work on each other with the techniques they have learnt. Even siblings of the unwell child can be taught some of the techniques so that they do not feel left out. Furthermore, sometimes the unwell child him- or herself may want to learn some of the techniques and will relish the opportunity to reciprocate with parents and siblings.

However, some important points should be noted:

- Complementary therapies are not a replacement for conventional medical care. Integrating complementary therapies and conventional medical care promotes a synergistic impact on the person's health and well-being.
- All complementary therapies are not safe in all circumstances. When considering safety, it is important to assess how the therapy will interact with the person's health condition; with the conventional treatments being received; and with any other complementary therapies being used. To this end, it is important to inform medical professionals of any complementary therapies being utilized and the complementary therapist of all the medical treatments being received, and remember to notify each professional of changes in treatments being provided by other professionals. It is also important to consider any possible side effects of the complementary therapy.
- Make the therapy fun for the child and encourage him or her to become involved in the process, so that it does not become just another tedious treatment.
- To find a therapist relevant to the therapy you want, contact the appropriate therapy governing body, many of which have the facility to find a therapist in your local area who is registered with them. Ensure that the therapist is insured to practise that particular therapy.

Organizations

Three major national organizations are described below, followed by an example of a local organization. Appendix 1 has contact details for these and a wide range of other organizations.

Association for Children's Palliative Care (ACT) – Katrina McNamara-Goodger, Head of Policy and Practice

ACT is a UK-wide charity working to achieve the best possible quality of life and care for every baby, child and young person who is not expected to reach adulthood. We raise awareness about what families and children need, help professionals to deliver the best possible care and support, and provide families with information and help. ACT also provides a range of publications and tools to help inform and support professionals and families in the development of best practice. ACT believes that families should have a choice of place of care, choice of social opportunities, choice of place of death and choice of emotional, psychological and bereavement support. Services should aim to help children and their families achieve a 'good' life and a 'good' death, and barriers should be removed to enable the child and family to lead as 'ordinary' a life as possible. ACT developed the first integrated care pathway (ICP) for children and young people with life-threatening or life-limiting conditions and their families.

Child Death Helpline

Calls to the Child Death Helpline are answered by a bereaved parent and callers may be anyone affected by a child's death, however long ago, in whatever circumstances. For those supporting families after the death of a child it can be useful to suggest the helpline as an adjunct to any other support that is being offered. Often, in the first weeks and months following a child's or young adult's death, many bereaved parents feel they cannot continue to burden others. They find it very beneficial to talk to someone who is impartial, has some understanding of their day-to-day struggle, and recognizes their need to retell the story of their child's death even though others may appear to want them to 'get over it' and return to normal. We also receive calls from people whose child died many years ago but who have issues they now want to talk through. What we *are* able to do is be alongside our callers, lessening their sense of isolation and encouraging them to give expression to whatever their thoughts may be. Those who are providing support may call the helpline too, simply to offload or to seek suggestions for other resources; we try to signpost to local agencies where these are available.

Child Bereavement Charity (CBC) – Ann Rowland, Director of Bereavement Services

The charity's vision is for all bereaved children and grieving families to have access to relevant support and information from appropriately trained professionals. The charity provides support and information to all affected by the death of a baby or child or when children are bereaved, and offers accessible training and support for the professionals who work with these families and children. CBC's interactive website provides a wide range of information to support professionals in their work with bereaved children and families. It offers free downloadable articles, resources and a professionals' forum to provide a space for professionals working in the field to raise questions or seek peer support. Our national telephone and email support line offers information to professionals and can signpost to resources, other appropriate national organizations or local bereavement support available in all areas of the UK. It also offers a national telephone support line to parents and other family members and an online families' forum, which provides a place to share experiences and feelings and to make contact with other bereaved parents and families. Parents who can travel to our national base in

Buckinghamshire can access individual or couple bereavement support sessions or bereavement support groups with other parents. Children in the family can access family support sessions or family peer support group meetings to provide opportunities for all family members to express their feelings through play and creative activities, and to meet and share with others.

Beyond the Horizon – Jeanette Rawlinson

Spurgeon's Beyond the Horizon works with children, young people and their families, meeting their grief needs through providing individual counselling, group support, family support, activity-day events, occasional outings and training in bereavement awareness to other professionals. When we are approached by the parent, carer or child, or by another professional with the permission of the parent, we arrange to meet initially with the parent or carer to talk about the loss and the changes this has made to the family and the child that has been referred to us. This helps parents to access the support they feel they need and identifies any other family members needing help. It is an opportunity to help parents to seek advice, guidance and reassurance on how they are supporting their child, to have a listening ear to offload their own concerns to and to help them feel less isolated. The parent and child are both involved in the decision-making about what support they would like, and a relationship with either the worker making a visit, a parent worker or a counsellor will begin. Families are made aware that our service is open to young people until they reach age 18, and so if the young person is not ready to access our help they know they can change their minds at any time. In these circumstances we often support the parent to support the child; it also helps the young person to feel in control of what is happening to him or her.

At our first visit families are left with appropriate leaflets and materials to help support them when we are not with them. These are also helpful if they decide they do not need our support. Parents are given information about our service and how to contact us, and information about what counselling is, how it is delivered and that we are an open-access service offering open-ended sessions – that is, the child decides when he or she no longer needs our support. We also leave a letter for the child and a booklet we have produced, called *Sam's Diary*, which explains our service in child-friendly language, together with a slip for the child to indicate whether he or she would like to meet someone to talk to and a stamped addressed envelope so children can make their own response. Young people are reassured at all times that it is their choice to accept our support and we actively work to ensure their choices are heard and responded to.

Our counsellors all receive supervision and support to ensure their own emotional health in working with the traumatic stories some children are dealing with. The counsellors take responsibility for their own professional development and this is supported by our organization with many opportunities to access further training and support.

Conclusion

This chapter has sought to offer some insights from professionals involved in palliative and bereavement care in the community. The intention has been to make carers aware of the resources that might be available to families, and to equip them with the information they need should families choose to discuss some of the issues with them.

For reflection

- What new organizations have you become aware of through reading this chapter? What new ideas has it given you?
- Do you have a list of local or accessible resources that you can give to parents?
- Are those involved in pastoral care in your church aware of the range of resources and agencies to which they can refer people?
- Do you have resources to offer local schools if they suffer the loss of a child?

8

Ethical issues

Imagine these scenarios:

- An eight-year-old child is dying at home but the parents do not want to tell him that he will die soon. They ask you what they should do.
- A child has been diagnosed with a condition which means she will not recover. The family ask you, 'Should we turn off the machine so our child does not suffer any more?'
- A member of your church, who has a child with a life-limiting, potentially life-threatening disease, refuses to let the child have any more treatment because she has prayed and has heard God tell her the child will be healed. How should you respond?

Rarely a week goes by without a story in the news about how people are dying when they don't want to or want to die when they can't – war, assisted suicide, accidents, murder, death and dying are on our television screens and in our newspapers on a daily basis. With some stories there is an ethical dimension, and that is an important part of this book, although one which is difficult to deal with because the law changes, government guidelines change and medical procedures develop and improve.

In this chapter I cannot possibly cover in any detail the breadth of ethical issues that arise – it would take many books to do this. What I want to do is headline and signpost some of the key concepts and elements so we can be better equipped to deal with such issues when they arise. I will provide background information as to how decisions are made in hospital and in the local community and offer some tools to equip you in your own work. I do not expect you to necessarily agree with all of my values, principles or conclusions, nor do I offer them as better than anyone else's; they are illustrative of what can be used and I would encourage you to think through your own.

A brief introduction to ethics

To say something is ethical is a meaningless phrase. Why do I say that? Well, when we look at the spectrum of ethical theory, we can quickly see that almost any action can be deemed ethical when it is justified from a particular stance. For instance, euthanasia can be called ethical if it is justified on the grounds of the greatest good for the greatest number of people. If we let a few people be killed so that the extraordinary amount of resources spent on those few can be spent on a lot more people, we might then say that, logically, euthanasia is ethical. Now many of us, including me, do not agree with euthanasia, but we need to be able to articulate why.

The idea of what is ethical is perhaps most used currently in relation to such things as climate change and food shopping. However, choices are rarely straightforward. Do I buy green beans from Africa because growing such produce provides an income for people without many alternatives, or do I not, because of the impact of flying food around the world? Medical ethics is sometimes like this too. Put simply, there are three main approaches to ethics:

- consequentialism – making decisions based on what the outcome is likely to be;
- deontologicalism – making decisions based on what is the right thing to do;
- virtue – making decisions based on what type of person I want to be.

Defining 'ethics' is not always easy as it can be confused with words such as 'morals'. A simple definition may be that:

- morals are the standards we have, and
- ethics are the ways in which we seek to reach these standards.

So for instance, morally, the standard by which I drive is that I will not drive above 30 miles an hour in a built-up area. Ethically, how have I reached this position? I could say: the law says I should not, so I don't. My Scriptures tell me to obey the law, so I obey it (deontologicalism). But the other reason, if I am really honest, is that I have been influenced by the adverts on TV that show how children are killed by speed (consequentialism), and also I want to be a courteous driver (virtue).

Today we live in a world and culture of such things as human rights and patients' charters. These have been set in place to ensure that high standards are aimed for and that abuses, like those that may have occurred in the past, do not happen again. This works for me because I like the way it emphasizes both sides – the patient and family and the hospital.

We all have resources we use in making ethical decisions regardless of what theoretical approach we may favour. There are five key resources:

- already developed norms, rules and laws, and using them as guiding lights;
- our ability to reason and act rationally, which involves evaluating the actions that will do as much good as possible and how to avoid doing harm;
- our conscience, which can act as an inner compass and an emotional indicator about what might make us feel good or bad;
- our capacity to empathize and in so doing put ourselves in someone else's place;
- our relationships with others as a source of advice, as sounding boards and as a source of comfort.

(Einhorn, cited in Ghaye, 2007, p. 155)

Table 8.1 overleaf provides an introduction to the main ways of making ethical decisions and suggests strengths and weaknesses of each approach.

Factors and dynamics in families' ethical decision-making

When families are faced with ethical issues relating to the care of their child a wide range of factors come into play. These include:

- *Deferment and power* Some families find it difficult to challenge the views of medical professionals and will have a tendency to defer to them as the specialists. It can also feel as if all the power is on the side of the professionals, who have the capacity to go to court to try and get their view upheld at the extreme end of disagreement.
- *Ignorance of issues* Many will be unaware of all the issues involved in particular situations, and it is here that online research and contacting organizations that offer support for particular diseases can be useful.
- *Incapacity by enormity* There are times when the issues seem so overwhelming that it is difficult to even begin to process them.
- *Pressure from extended family* Sometimes parents are faced with conflicting advice from extended family members who may have clear ideas of what should be done. When I do an emergency baptism it can sometimes feel that the grandparents' wish for it to happen has taken precedence.
- *Cultural expectations* Can come into play in respect of such issues as who in the family takes the decision or how one sees the will of God in the circumstances.
- *Capacity* Some medical issues are so complex it can be really hard to understand the details and the way this is then translated into treatment choices, for example. For some, either educational or emotional issues may make it hard for them to make a decision.

Table 8.1 Approaches to making ethical decisions

Criterion	*Strengths*	*Weaknesses*
Consequences (teleological, e.g. utilitarianism, which proposes the greatest good for the greatest number of people)	Facilitates calculating the outcomes and making comparisons Focuses on outcomes Congruent with traditional outcome-oriented evaluation	Difficult to assess effects on everybody affected May result in restricting someone's rights Difficult to define what is good and whose goods take the priority
Duty (deontological, e.g. Kant's categorical imperative: all persons should act as if their actions were to become universal)	Provides a clear picture of expectations Takes contractual and professional relationships into consideration	May overemphasize managerial perspectives May neglect the needs of stakeholders
Rights (a positive right suggests that someone has an obligation to act in a certain way; a negative right suggests that someone has an obligation to refrain from acting in a certain way)	Provides minimal protection for individuals Separates behavioural standards from the outcomes	May fail to consider social justice issues Rights are not absolute and they may conflict
Social justice (e.g. Rawls' equal access – equal right to basic liberties – but supports unequal distribution if it assists the least well-off as that will then benefit society as a whole)	Ensures that goods are allocated fairly	May emphasize entitlement at the expense of effort or creativity May restrict some stakeholder rights Changes the traditional role of the evaluator from a neutral observer to an advocate
Ethics of care (emphasizes the importance of considering how particular individuals, human relationships and institutions would be affected by the alternative choices available)	Takes specific contexts into account Examines effect on relationships	May appear relativistic Difficult to determine whose care is the most pertinent

(Newman and Brown, cited in Huotari, 2003, pp. 125–7)

Ministerial ethics

Much of the material in previous chapters is relevant here in terms of values and principles but these are core to my approach:

- to act with love and compassion towards the child and the family;
- to act with integrity and in line with any denominational or organizational guidelines;
- to be intentionally available and vulnerable with families;
- to be quick to be present and listen, and slow to speak and judge;
- to respond and work with the needs of the family and not be manipulative;
- to leave my own stuff at home;
- to integrate into the community where possible;
- to refer when necessary.

One way of doing ethics is Kant's categorical imperative, which involves only doing what we wish everyone to do, and if I had to work with such a construct I would end up with:

- to always be compassionate and loving;
- to always listen and be fully present.

Medical ethics

Common ethical dilemmas and issues

I am the vice-chair of the Clinical Ethics Committee at BCH. The Committee's aims and objectives are 'to provide a forum for confidential multidisciplinary discussion and analysis of matters of ethical concern arising from clinical practice at BCH and to provide, where appropriate, an informed, reasoned and justifiable opinion or commentary on such matters'. We offer advice only on:

1 ethical issues arising from clinical cases, prospectively and retrospectively;
2 the education of ethics advisory group members and Trust staff in relevant bioethical issues;
3 assisting the development of institutional guidance that involves clinical ethical issues.

The type of issues that regularly arise are:

- end of life, e.g. where should the child die?
- consent, e.g. who gives consent, what about when there is disagreement?
- refusal of treatment, e.g. for religious reasons;

- withholding or withdrawing treatment, e.g. when is this point reached, who decides and how?
- confidentiality, e.g. what information is needed, who is it shared with and how?
- human rights, e.g. what rights are there to particular treatments?
- organ donation, e.g. criteria around who should get an organ and how this is decided;
- other issues, such as having another child so he or she can donate to the sick sibling, gene and stem cell research, etc.

We may have to support families making decisions in all these areas.

Legal dimensions

There is not space here to go into all the legal and ethical issues facing children and their families. Helpful internet resources for this include: the NHS Choices website, <www.nhs.uk/Pages/HomePage.aspx>, which is a starting point for gaining information; a helpful summary of issues surrounding consent and children and young people at <www.patient.co.uk/doctor/Consent-to-Treatment-in-Children.htm>; and the Ethox website, <www.ethox.org.uk>, which has information about a lot of different ethical issues, including a helpful handout on end of life and the law.

I want, however, to mention one specific situation. We increasingly hear stories on the news of hospitals and families going to court to achieve their objectives. The hospital and the family will have tried to find a common agreement, and most of the time this happens. When it does not, resorting to the courts can be initiated by either party. Hospitals will have access to legal advice and will have sought this before taking a case further. This usually occurs when the family and the hospital:

- do not agree on the treatment of the child;
- have a breakdown in communication;
- have a breakdown of trust;
- have different definitions of what is in the best interest of the child.

Bearison notes that

> Sometimes it is paediatricians who are reluctant to accept medical futility and shift from curative intent to palliative care and comfort. However, most times when paediatricians and parents are not on the same page it is the parents who are unable to accept when enough is enough and, consequently, resist appropriate palliative care and sedation.
>
> (2006, pp. 157–8)

Ethical principles used in making decisions in the treatment of children

There are four widely accepted principles in medical ethics:

- autonomy – the opportunity to act, think and make choices freely while respecting the rights of others to autonomy;
- non-maleficence – not causing undue harm or inflicting evil;
- beneficence – doing good to others;
- resource allocation and justice.

These are found in most of the literature and are core to the way that decisions are made. Beauchamp and Childress (2001) also identify four virtues which they think are pertinent to the character of health professionals and so make a contribution to ethical decision-making. These are compassion, discernment, trustworthiness and integrity. Thus, these virtues should underpin decisions made and help us to understand the perspective of medical professionals. Campbell advocates that a combination of the four principles and virtue ethics offers a more rounded approach to making ethical decisions: 'Virtue ethics directs us to the character of the decision maker, but also to the implications for our whole lives and for society of individual choices and policy decisions' (cited in Gill, 2006, p. 103).

Many of the principles used and applied in medical ethics are compatible with Christianity and are drawn from and influenced by our faith. Such principles as not causing harm, being good stewards of limited resources, seeking justice and fairness and being honest are all in keeping with Christianity.

As we discuss cases brought to us at our ethics advisory group, my observation is that we apply the principle of best interest more than all the other principles. This is because as a hospital, we have the child, as our patient, as our primary concern. We ask ourselves, 'If these are the options, which one is best for the child? Which will cause the least pain, bring about the best outcome?' So parents can be assured their child is foremost in our minds as we offer advice. It is interesting to reflect on how we work this out in the context of the needs and opinions of their wider family and community.

Resource allocation – another elephant in the room

There is one principle of care that is among the most difficult, and that is resource allocation. It is the ethical 'elephant in the room' that very few people, including politicians, want to talk about as it is very emotive. When we consider that there is not a limitless amount of money to provide limitless operations, procedures and numbers of beds, it is easy – and, I would suggest, justifiable – to see why it is an awkward area to discuss. Some of the relevant issues here are:

- the guidelines of the National Institute for Health and Clinical Excellence (NICE) on acceptable treatments, drugs, etc.;
- funding and commissioning;
- the number of medical interventions;
- targets to be met, ratings;
- available equipment, staff numbers and specialisms;
- numbers of available beds, particularly in intensive care;
- the availability of ancillary services that can enhance well-being in hospital, such as chaplaincies, that have hard-to-measure outcomes.

This is an area with which the general public are becoming more and more familiar as stories of hospital budgets are discussed in the public arena. Foundation hospitals, such as BCH, give a good opportunity for the wider community to be involved in local hospitals, ensuring that accountability and transparency are at the core of healthcare. This must be good news.

Processes for dealing with ethical dilemmas in healthcare

There are processes designed to help ethicists and practitioners to process an ethical dilemma. They do not appeal to everyone – some find them restrictive in creative problem-solving – but I find them helpful for two reasons. First, they ensure thoroughness in taking all the factors into account, and second, they help support and give security to those who are first stepping out in this field. The method I advocate using is the Jonsen Framework, where the following questions are worked through in order:

1 *Indications for medical intervention* What is the diagnosis, what are the options for treatment, what are the prognoses for each of the options?
2 *Preferences of patient* Is the patient competent? If so, what does he or she want? If not competent, then what is in the patient's best interest?
3 *Quality of life* Will the proposed treatment improve the patient's quality of life?
4 *Contextual features* Do religious, cultural, legal factors have an impact on the decision? (Jonsen *et al.*, 1992)

What might Christians add in making ethical decisions?

The term 'wisdom' may be something we want to add to the idea of knowledge. Perhaps wisdom is knowledge applied mindfully. Prayer is also missing, and it is always possible for people of faith to pray silently if they are involved in a situation when to pray out loud may be perceived as inappropriate. One of the ways I have sought to address this in a group is to invite participants to take a moment of quiet before we come to a decision or finish our meeting. I present it as a reflective space and practice, and some people have commented how helpful this has been. I may be praying and so may others, but it gives space to everyone without being in danger of being offensive. I normally go on to offer people the opportunity to share anything else they may not have yet said.

There are also theological perspectives to take into account. I often wonder, when taking part in an ethical debate on what advice should be given, how the outcome might be different if all those involved were Christians and believed the child was made in the image of God and going to heaven if he or she died. Gill suggests that compassion

> offers a critique of a number of positions in Christian ethics, especially those involved in 'status of life' issues. All too often Christian interventions in the public forum on these issues appear to have been more concerned with maintaining principled scruples than with starting (like the Synoptic Jesus) from compassion. Although a commitment to compassion does not in itself resolve dilemmas in health care ethics, it does suggest priorities.
> (2006, pp. 104–5)

A way forward

Having explored a range of issues around making ethical decisions in palliative and bereavement care, the challenge is what to do now! Here are some suggestions:

- Offer training sessions on making ethical decisions.
- Hold debates or discussions around medical ethical issues.
- Find out about your local ethics advisory group (EAG).
- Invite a local chaplain to come and talk about the work of the group.
- Offer to join a local EAG as a lay person – most groups are looking for lay people to join.
- Join the hospital foundation – all foundation trusts offer this opportunity.
- Consider a preaching or small group series on ethics.

Ethics will only become more complex with advances in medicine and changing family patterns, and it may be that one of the most significant tools we can equip ourselves and others with is the ability to make sound ethical decisions.

For reflection

- What are the medical ethical issues in your own context? What new tools do you have to address them?
- What are your ministerial ethical principles and values for your visiting?
- What are the imperatives that work for you?
- How do you help your congregation to process ethical decisions?
- Look at the list of ideas under 'A way forward' in the previous section. Which seem most practical for your context?

9

Services, rituals and blessings

> To live in the hearts of those we leave behind is not to die.
>
> (Inscription on a headstone in Lytham St Anne's)

> My experience of losing Kasey-Jayne has not been easy. I suppose being able to do her foot and handprints was helpful, and taking a lock of hair while she was still alive helped, but what killed me the most was looking into her eyes and her looking like she was in so much pain and that she couldn't fight any more. I spent every day with my daughter and the night before she came home and spent the night with her family and on the day of her funeral I got her dressed for her special day and placed her into her coffin. I was the last one to kiss her and hold her and no one can ever take that from me.

This chapter will explore principles, best practice, questions and reflections behind the rituals and services we may use in palliative and bereavement care, as well as providing examples of resources; further examples are on the BCH website, and many of the resources can be used in a range of contexts. I encourage everyone in ministry not to be uncritical when assessing the materials and approaches we use. This is an important area. As Staudacher writes, 'Modern western society is severely deficient in its treatment of death. In contrast, many other cultures have definite rituals, which promote the exhibition of emotion and provide adequate time for mourning' (1987, p. 10).

Why children's funerals and memorials are difficult

I have been conducting funerals for children and young people for a while now and I still struggle. They are just very difficult, and these are some of the reasons why:

- In the natural order of life the occasion should not be happening.
- The expectations of the family are for it to be perfect.
- There is tension within the objectives – a time to grieve but also a time to celebrate.
- There may be a lack of suitable resources.
- There may be tension within the family dynamics and a multiple level of connectedness to the child.

- There may be delays or problems arising out of the nature of the death.
- There may be contributing factors to the death.
- There may be lack of agreement in the family about what is wanted.

There are some differences in the difficulties depending on the child's age and cause of death. However, some of the difficulties are of our own making. Sometimes we seek to achieve inappropriate objectives using unsuitable materials. Funerals and memorials need to be well thought through and we need to consider how the material we usually use may be heard.

Nick Ball, BCH chaplain, reflects on taking a child's funeral:

Most of the families for whom I have conducted funerals have been anxious that the service should be about their child rather than something generalized. Some families do not feel confident enough to get up and tell their child's story themselves, but want you to. One family had produced an occasional bulletin, complete with photographs, of their child's short life journey, and this was a wonderful resource in preparing the address. Some families want to write their own tribute, but do not know where to start. Twice I have lent families another parent's tribute to give families a model. On one occasion I read the tribute they produced, on another occasion a member of the family read it. Even with a neonatal death a member of the family may wish to speak. An Australian father spoke very movingly about all the things that he and his partner never got the chance to do with their baby, such as dangling his toes in the sea.

Some parents will choose a poem: there are a number on the internet, but it is useful to take a selection with you when you visit. Other parents will write a poem, which they will either want to read themselves or get the minister to read. Some parents aren't sure if they will be able to manage to read on the day. I always tell them that they probably will manage, but that if they can't they can give it to me and I will read it. Of course, ministers can choke themselves, especially if they have known the child well. Underlying this is the parents' desire to do all that they can for their child. They will often feel guilty that they have failed to protect their child from mortality; they will want to be sure that in death they have done all that they could.

Theological rationale for liturgical activities

When approaching liturgy for palliative and bereavement care it's helpful to have an underpinning theological rationale. This helps you understand what you are and are not doing and helps with the selection of material and the structure of the act. Nick Ball suggests that the theology of the service should be simple and clear, and where possible it should be earthed in something that can be seen. The baptism candle can be a very good symbol to preach around. The idea of God holding the child safe is powerful – we have a little statue of a child being held in the palm of a hand, which is clearly meant to be God's hand. If other symbols are used, dwelling on their meaning for a little while may be an effective way of communicating.

People of lament

When coming alongside children and families, we do this as people of faith but also as real human beings. In our rituals and services we seek to honour not only the child but also the pain the families feel. To lament is to cry out in anguish, to acknowledge the pain, grief, loss and 'bereft-ment' – it is so very real and is important to express. This is not the opposite of faith: this is faith. I do not come with a quick 'All will be well'; I come alongside to say, with the family, 'This is not well, this is horrible.' My reflection is that some Christians are not comfortable with this approach because it seems to express a lack of faith in God, along with issues previously explored of seeing this as the will of God. This is not to say we whip people up to a mourning frenzy, but it does mean we give and create space and opportunity to express sorrow with affirmation and without condemnation.

A poem several parents have shared as being significant has elements of lament:

> I am wearing a pair of shoes.
> They are ugly shoes.
> Uncomfortable shoes.
> I hate my shoes.
> Each day I wear them, and each day I wish I had another pair.
> Some days my shoes hurt so bad that I do not think I can take
> another step.
> Yet, I continue to wear them.
> I get funny looks wearing these shoes.
> They are looks of sympathy.
> I can tell in others' eyes that they are glad they are my shoes and
> not theirs.
> They never talk about my shoes.
> To learn how awful my shoes are might make them uncomfortable.
> To truly understand these shoes you must walk in them.
> But, once you put them on, you can never take them off.
> I now realize that I am not the only one who wears these shoes.
> There are many pairs in the world.

Some women are like me and ache daily as they try and walk in them.
Some have learned how to walk in them so they don't hurt quite
as much.
Some have worn the shoes so long that days will go by
before they think of how much they hurt.
No woman deserves to wear these shoes.
Yet, because of the shoes I am a stronger woman.
These shoes have given me the strength to face anything.
They have made me who I am.
I will forever walk in the shoes of a woman who has lost a child.
(Anon)

Resurrection as process

It can be helpful to encourage the idea of seeing resurrection as a process rather than just a one-off event. Sometimes it will feel that the new life after bereavement is a speck on the furthest horizon and it will take a long journey to get there. Hope does come in the morning – we are just not sure which morning. In our prayers and rituals, we do not seek to rush people to a place of being immediately reconciled to the outcome, but to sit with them in whatever sense of death or life after death they are in. This prayer may be helpful in expressing some of the Christian hope:

You shared life with us, God give eternal life to you.
You gave your love to us, God give his deep love to you.
You gave your time to us, God give his eternity to you.
You gave your light to us, God give everlasting light to you.
Go upon your journey, dear soul, to love, light and life eternal.
(Source unknown, cited in Wilson with McCreary, 2001, p. 115)

Pastoral expediency versus theological integrity – dealing with faith and culture

This can be a tension when working out the content of the order of service for a funeral. What do we do when the family want a song or a poem we feel is very inappropriate as a reflection of the Christian message? My suggestion is to work with it. A good question to ask ourselves at this point is 'Why am I so offended? God's reputation or mine?' Taste is often culturally determined and meaning is important in a funeral; usually material is chosen because it has a personal meaning for the family. There are many generational and cultural differences in the way that people respond to bereavement and the way they want to remember their child.

Having said that, I do have some concerns about certain readings I have heard and been asked to use. One example is Henry Scott Holland's 'Death is nothing at all'. There are many reasons why I think this is unsuitable for a child's funeral. First, it's a lie: it contains the line 'all is well'. Second, the poem belittles death. I appreciate its sentiment and the fact that it is written by a minister and focuses on the promise of a life ongoing: it is important to have hope in the resurrection, to know that the child is safe and to be assured that in time we will be reunited with our loved ones but, that said, the poem continues to encourage an attitude that everything is all right because you will see your loved one again. It is not all right – it's a tragedy. Death is everything to parents who have lost their first, fifth or only child.

This is another example of a piece of writing that I have heard read at the funeral of a child:

> A beautiful story is told of a devout Christian home in which there were twin boys who were greatly beloved. In the absence of the father, both boys suddenly died. When the father returned, not knowing the sorrow in his home, the mother met him at the door and said, 'I have had a strange visitor since you went away.'
>
> 'Who was it?' asked the father.
>
> 'Five years ago,' his wife answered, 'a Friend lent me two precious jewels. Yesterday he came and asked me to return them to him. What shall I do?'
>
> 'Are they his?' asked the father, not dreaming of her meaning.
>
> 'Yes, they belong to him and were only lent to me.'
>
> 'If they are his, he must have them again if he desires.'
>
> Leading her husband to the boys' room, the wife drew down the sheet, uncovering the lovely forms, white as marble. 'These are my jewels,' said the mother. 'Five years ago God lent them to me, and yesterday he came and asked for them again. What shall we do?'
>
> With a great sob, the father said, bowing his head, 'The will of the Lord be done.'

I have reflected on such theology in previous chapters. It causes me a real dilemma if I am asked to read such a piece. I now have the courage and conviction to suggest other pieces of writing, but if the family are keen I do not let it get as far as a refusal. I would be willing to include it in the service and I may even read it myself out of pastoral concern for the family.

In conclusion, my advice is to pick your battles wisely. At least I have not had a request to play 'My way' at a child's funeral. Well, not yet anyway!

Principles for developing and delivering services

I want to explore some key principles that need to be borne in mind when planning services or rituals.

Be prepared

Prepare yourself for what you are likely to encounter

This is core to everything: we need to prepare ourselves emotionally and spiritually for what we will be doing. We should remember that God is with us, indeed has gone before us. We should expect many of the elements of loss and grief that we explored in Chapter 1. If we expect the unexpected, we will nearly always be ready. In a funeral visit a family may have the whole service laid out with some bizarre (to us) suggestions of music to come in and out to. I am sometimes less prepared for a family to be matter-of-fact in their grief and very reasonable about what they want in the funeral. I am certainly concerned when the family are immobilized and therefore apathetic.

Prepare to be shocked

As well as the power of the emotions and reactions of the family, there are also other aspects that can be shocking. The size of the coffin can be a real shock, to you and to others – some of them are so tiny, it is hard to believe there is someone inside. Emotions run high; people sometimes say things they later regret or family feuds that had been patched up can break out again.

If we go prepared to be shocked, we should also go with the intention of not showing that shock.

Balance who you are with what you say and what you do

One of the main fears in doing any end-of-life or death liturgy is saying the wrong thing. I was invited to our diocesan liturgy group meeting to discuss this topic and the point was made that, while what we say is important, who we are with and to the bereaved family is perhaps more important. However, always ensure you know the name of the child, the name that child was known by and the names of parents or significant others. If you make a mistake, apologize and move on.

Name the pain and the emotions

We obviously take some of our lead from the family, but sometimes it feels as though there is an elephant in the room that nobody is prepared to name. There are times when we need to be the ones who name it. This is a saying I often use:

> All day long, singing,
> yet the day's not long enough
> for the skylark's song.
>
> (Basho, seventeenth-century haiku, translator unknown, from <http://scriptorpress.yage.net/BM36_2004_basho.pdf>)

I really like this for several reasons, but mostly because it seeks to balance the celebration and sadness of the life and death of a child. It encapsulates the tension felt at many end-of-life and bereavement occasions, that the young person or child was wonderful while he or she was with us and that we wish it had been for longer. I like the honesty of it.

Take some resources with you

Like a lot of ministers I always take a list of readings, songs and poems with me when I visit a family. I have a small booklet with an order of service in it, with options for prayers, blessings, etc., to choose from depending on what I sense is appropriate at the time. I almost always share the 'Footprints' poem with a family as a prayer for them:

> One night I had a dream.
> I dreamed I was walking along the beach with God,
> And across the sky flashed scenes from my life.
> For each scene I noticed two sets of footprints in the sand;
> One belonged to me and the other to God.
> When the last scene of my life flashed before me
> And I looked back at the footprints in the sand,
> I noticed that at times along the path of life
> There was only one set of footprints.
> I also noticed that it happened
> At the very lowest and saddest times of my life.
> This really bothered me
> And I questioned God about it.
> 'God, you said that once I decided to follow you,
> You would walk with me all the way,
> But I noticed that during the most troublesome times in my life
> There is only one set of footprints.
> I do not understand why, in times when I needed you most, you would leave me.'
> God replied, 'My precious child,
> I love you and I would never leave you
> During your times of trials and suffering.
> When you see only one set of footprints,
> It was then that I carried you.'

I find this resource almost universally helpful in my pastoral work, and give out professionally printed copies including the chaplaincy contact details; these are now easy to obtain and reasonably priced online. The story cuts to the heart of God's love for the family and expresses the Christian understanding of where God is and how he wants to relate to the bereaved. When I am asked to take the funeral, I am often asked to read 'Footprints'.

There may also be resources within the church or community that can be used. One of our chaplains, Pam Turner, writes poetry, and her poem 'Celebrating brief lives' works well at a child's funeral:

There, and gone:
full of golden promise
then
like a frail single petal
on a gorgeous flower-head
fallen –
fallen and blown by the wind
on a fluttering fairground ride to heaven
where
filigree fingers of silver-white light
catch and hold
her soul.

Empower the family

Before we meet with the family we need to think through the balance mentioned above between following the wishes of the family and ensuring a Christian ritual with dignity and faith. Sometimes the two seem a little incongruent. My belief is that we are there to help facilitate the family's wishes but that we should also share resources and ideas with them, ensuring that we are aware of any power dynamics and the propensity of people to agree with those they see as being in authority.

We may need to engage with folk religion and clichés in a timely sensitive way. Sometimes we just need to let it slide; on other occasions we may need to bring an orthodox Christian perspective into the conversation.

Some examples of what families have done for funerals

We had flowers made in the shape of Cameron's favourite teddy and some other people also had flowers made in the shape of his favourite TV character.

We had several poems as readings at the funeral as the words were very apt, and also two poems that I wrote for the funeral.

We had a song called 'Fly' by Celine Dion as the entrance music at the funeral because the words of the song are very apt – other families choose a favourite song of the child's.

We released red balloons when we came out of the funeral and into the gardens where the flowers had been laid out. The vicar read a poem first and then we released the balloons. It was a lovely end to the funeral and made it more childlike.

A member of our family organized memorial cards to be made for us to give to family and friends.

For the funeral we commissioned a coffin made of woven willow and ensured the undertaker would line it with the same fabric we'd used to make Willow's bedroom curtains. We tied beautiful ribbons and little bows all over to make it very girly and pretty. The floral arrangement incorporated a bunch of lavender which we'd picked from our garden. We all wrote farewell cards and Emily drew a picture – and we stuck special photos around the inside of the coffin and placed a couple of her favourite books in too.

We provided small cards for everyone to write down their personal memories.

Her ashes were placed in a beautiful ceramic pot that another friend made for us, and she now sleeps on a shelf above our bed surrounded by trinkets and baubles that we collected during her short life and still collect for her now.

Josie was having a discussion with her friend one day and she explained what she wanted for her funeral. She mapped it all out, songs, etc., so this is what we did.

We have a memorial stone for Jeremy and Nathan in a member of the family's garden, and vases for flowers which we take each time we go to our stone for the boys.

We had our child's name entered into the book of remembrance and we go to see this on the anniversary of his death.

A dove was released after the service and it flew to a tree, sat and watched us and then flew away.

Balance the needs of grief and thanksgiving

It never ceases to amaze me that even in the saddest and most tragic of circumstances in the death of a child, a family still has the capacity to give thanks for the gift of their child. It makes no difference how long or short the child's life has been. I have seen some families give thanks out of a need for redemptive motives but I have also seen gratitude expressed in healthy reflective grief. This poem picks up this tension:

You can shed tears that she is gone,
or you can smile because she has lived.
You can close your eyes and pray that she'll come back,
or you can open your eyes and see all she's left.
Your heart can be empty because you can't see her,
or you can be full of the love you shared.
You can turn your back on tomorrow and live yesterday,
or you can be happy for tomorrow because of yesterday.
You can remember only that she is gone,
or you can cherish her memory and let it live on.
You can cry and close your mind,
be empty and turn your back.
Or you can do what she'd want:
smile, open your eyes, love and go on. (Anon)

Encourage questions and discussion

The death of a child may be a time when people want to ponder some of the big questions of life. Encourage people to verbalize their questions and concerns and be prepared to engage in a discussion that is helping individuals process their thoughts and feelings.

Designing the service

Choice of liturgy

Common Worship contains a lot of good material, while some of the prayers in *Liturgies for Daily Life* (McRae-McMahon, 2004) can strike just the right note, especially for a neonatal funeral or that of a young child. For miscarriages and neonatal deaths the special service in the *Methodist Service Book* has a simplicity that can be powerful. One of our chaplains and his wife chose this service for the funeral of their son, who miscarried at 13 weeks. Liturgy that has a familiar element can be helpful too, like this 'Litany of remembrance' from Roland Gittelsohn (1975, p. 552):

In the rising of the sun and in its going down, we remember them.
In the blowing of the wind and in the chill of winter, we remember them.
In the opening of buds and in the rebirth of spring, we remember them.
In the blueness of the sky and in the warmth of summer, we remember them.
In the rustling of leaves and in the beauty of autumn, we remember them.
In the beginning of the year and when it ends, we remember them.

When we are weary and in need of strength, we remember them.
When we are lost and sick at heart, we remember them.
When we have joys we yearn to share, we remember them.
So long as we live, they too shall live, for they are now a part of us, as we remember them.

Be creative

I always try to make the funeral of a child memorable in some way and try to be creative in helping people in their grief journey. One of the things that I often use is gold hearts (small fabric ones usually) and I invite family members to come and take a heart and put it on the coffin as a symbol of their love. I may also have forget-me-nots there, too, which they take as a visual reminder of who they have lost. My colleague Nick Ball finds a focus on the baptism candle helpful. The child may have been given a baptism candle when (and if) he or she was baptized, although if baptism took place on a hospital ward this probably will not have happened. Lighting the child's baptism candle or lighting a new baptismal candle can be a very powerful symbol. It could be lit early in the service, after a reading that affirms eternal hope or after the address, with an appropriate prayer. It is best if the candle can be lit from a Paschal candle to reinforce the point that resurrection life comes through Christ's resurrection. If the child wasn't baptized a candle can still be lit.

This prayer is appropriate; the material in brackets is Nick's addition:

> Let us light a (tiny) candle as a symbol of this delicate life which was unable to stay alight and earthed among us (but which now shines in the eternal light of heaven). (McRae-McMahon, 2004)

Pick a theme

This might be a colour, a favourite hobby or the child's favourite character. It can help the service seem a little more accessible and reinforce the individuality of the event.

Think hard about your readings

I think we need to revisit our default readings for the funeral or memorial service for a child. I will often use Psalm 23, as this engages with both life and death and reassures us of God's presence even through the difficult times. I use it to affirm the child and family by saying that I believe that goodness and mercy has followed the child all the days of his or her life, however long or short. Another reason for using this reading is that it is still familiar to many, even if only as the theme tune to *The Vicar of Dibley*!

There are some readings I am concerned about. One is Jesus blessing the children, Matthew 19.13–15. Now why on earth would I not like one of the few verses that mentions Jesus and children in a positive light? Well, it's true that it does show Jesus in a good light in his attitude towards children, but does that mean it is suitable for a funeral? Let's look at the key verse in the passage. Jesus said, 'Let the little children come to me' (v. 14). Now read this again and think about a person representing God standing up at the front of a funeral and saying these words. What do we think a grieving family might hear? Are we not in danger of reinforcing the suggestion that God has taken their child, that he wants the child to be with him rather than here on earth?

Singing and music

I have almost as much difficulty picking hymns and songs for funerals as I do Bible readings. So many of them are full of attitudes more appropriate for an adult's death, or even profess victory in death, and do not engage with the injustice of the death of a child. The hymns I am most frequently asked for are 'All things bright and beautiful' and 'Morning has broken'. I tend to think that they are chosen because they are familiar from school or because the family want a child-friendly song. Nick Ball's experience is that some families want hymns or worship songs while others will want recorded music in the service, often music that was the child's particular favourite. Some families will want both, and others will want a small service without music. Music at 'graveside only' burials, which are common with contract funerals, is difficult, but I do have a battery-powered CD player which can be used even in the rain. Some families will have very clear ideas about what they want; others will want a list of suggestions. One funeral I took ended with 'I love you, you love me' from *Barney*, which was a very appropriate message. I struggled a bit with 'Head, shoulders, knees and toes' at another service and said at the outset that I wasn't going to do the actions! My personal encouragement to the family is not to have too many hymns as singing is generally difficult.

There are very few hymns that have been written specifically for children's funerals or memorial services. This hymn is sung to the tune of 'Morning has broken' and we use it every year at our annual memorial service:

> Fleetingly known, yet ever remembered
> These are our children, now and always,
> These whom we see not, we will forget not,
> Morning and evening, all of our days.

Lives that touched our lives, tenderly, briefly,
Now in the one light living always,
Named in our hearts now, safe from all harm now,
We will remember all of our days.

As we recall them, silently name them,
Open our hearts, Lord, now and always,
Grant to us, grieving, love for the living,
Strength for each other, all of our days.

Safe in your peace, Lord, hold these our children,
Grace, light and laughter grant them each day,
Cherish and hold them 'til we may know them,
When in your glory we find our way.
(Author unknown)

Provide space

There should be some space in a funeral for people to reflect quietly on their loss. It may be while some music is playing or in short periods of silence between different parts of the funeral.

Give opportunity and permission for the expression of emotions

Many people go to funerals with the intention of holding it all together. This may be right for some but for others it is important to be able to release some of their emotions. Telling people what is okay can be helpful and making them feel comfortable in what for many is an unfamiliar environment can be important. And don't be afraid to use (gentle) humour. Using humour can release tension and help people to get into the service.

What are we seeking to achieve in the sermon?

My aim is to engage with the spectrum of emotions, such as grief, sorrow, regret, thankfulness, celebration, joy. I do not use all these themes in any one sermon but they are ideas I return to:

> To love and be loved. X knew what it was to love and was loved by others. These are the greatest gifts we have been given and have available to share with others. No matter how long X might have lived, [he or she] would not have experienced any greater gift in life.

This is often my first point. I use it to honour the family and what they gave the child but also to highlight what the family would have experienced. I have also decided not to shy away from talking about God's love for the child, as well as sometimes for the wider family members. At the same time, it may also be helpful to include in the sermon a reassurance that the child's suffering and death was not God's will, still less some form of punishment for that child or the family:

> This situation has nothing to do with what we deserve. Life is not fair. It has been said that suffering is hard enough, but senseless suffering is worse. What sense can we make of X's death? God did not want [him or her] to die. We live in a fallen world, and good things happen to evil people and evil things happen to good people. I do not believe God plans when we die, but he does know it is going to happen. I believe God is outside of time and has the capacity to look back in time. I believe he looks back at the death of your child and weeps. Our world is not how God planned or hoped. It is flawed, fragile, as are we human beings.

In conclusion, I encourage the family to go on, to continue to love and not to let this tragedy prevent them loving again. I seek to reassure them again of God's love for them and of the importance of processing the grief.

> X gave many gifts in life, and this is [his or her] gift to you all in [his or her] death: the opportunity to continue to love [him or her], to love others and to be loved yourself. There is no greater gift. A love that heals, releases fear, gives sacrificially, brings light into the darkness, hope into despair. [His or her] and Jesus' legacy is our free gift: love. As the family has found, love is the antidote to the pain, the ability in tragedy to love and be loved by others, to risk and reach out and care. In this we find we are transformed by suffering, not crippled by it. Love heals. To let others and God into our pain, anger and grief is not a dead end but a life-giving start. X has made the lives around [him or her] richer beyond measure. [He or she] accomplished so much in a short period of time. Your love for X goes on even when you do not understand. God's love for us and for X goes on in our sadness, anger, grief, confusion. Letting go is not betrayal. Love lives on and can get stronger as the pain becomes just a little less.

Leading services

In leading the service I seek to express the heart of God. It is a Christian funeral and I want to ensure that I fully emphasize this. I also seek to verbalize the hopes of the parents that their child is now at peace and pain free.

Cover the spectrum of feeling in the prayers

The purpose of the prayers is to communicate God's love for both the child and the family, to convey hope and support, as in this prayer from *Common Worship*:

> God of all comfort and grace, we thank you for the gift and life of X.
> We thank you we are all made in your image.
> We thank you for the place X held and still holds in our lives.
> We thank you for the love [he or she] gave.
> We remember the good times and the not so good times,
> the times of laughter and of tears.

We thank you for the love that was given, received, shared.
We thank you that your love for [him or her] and us
goes on in life and in death
and this is something we can imitate you in.
You know our thoughts and pain this day.
Be with us and lead us out of our desolation.
Bring peace where there is worry.
Bring calm where there is anguish.
Comfort this family with your presence and love.
Be with them and help ease their pain and bereavement.
Help them to find assurance
that nothing with you needs to be wasted.
Help us now to have the courage and strength
to leave them in your care.
We pray these things in and through the name of Jesus
who loves us and died for us.
Amen. (*Common Worship*)

I do not use the Lord's Prayer any more unless it is available for all participants to read. I have been in too many services where it has been assumed the congregation will know it. I do not think this honours the prayer, and it encourages a feeling of exclusion where the complete opposite needs to be facilitated. There is also the dilemma of which version to use; many churches use a modern version, but those who have a memory of saying it in the past tend to recall the traditional version.

Be multigenerational

It is more than just the parents who are impacted by the death of a child. Grandparents and others will also be facing the loss and their pain should be acknowledged also, as should that of siblings.

Be courageous

I pray about each funeral that I take, and if I have a sense of the Holy Spirit leading me in a particular way then I seek to follow that. Sometimes it takes courage to say something when you don't always know what the response might be.

Let some of the content of the ritual do the talking

We don't always need to spell out what we are doing or why we are doing it. Sometimes actions speak louder than words.

Encourage the family to say goodbye

However many times I lead an end-of-life blessing or do a funeral, I am never comfortable when it comes to encouraging the family to say goodbye. That is not to say I do not have the deepest conviction that it is important, because I do. My dilemma is that I cannot imagine how a family summon up the ability to say goodbye to their child. When I do an end-of-life blessing for a child, I always encourage the family to do two things:

- Speak to children as though they can understand every word you are saying. Leave nothing unsaid. Tell them how much you love them, how much you miss them and that you will never forget them.
- When the time comes, say goodbye. This, I find, is done in stages:
  (a) while the child is still alive;
  (b) on visits to see the child in the bereavement suite at the hospital or the funeral home;
  (c) at the funeral;
  (d) at the burial or scattering of ashes.

This is a commissioning and blessing that I use. I love the beauty of the flow of words, the rhythm, the imagery:

> To you, gentle Father,
> we humbly entrust this child so precious in your sight.
> Take [him or her] into your arms
> and welcome [him or her] into your presence
> where there is no sorrow nor pain,
> but the fullness of peace and joy with you
> for ever and ever. [All say] Amen.
>
> (Adapted from *Common Worship*)

> X, go forth from this world:
> in the love of God the Father who created you,
> in the mercy of Jesus Christ who redeemed you,
> in the power of the Holy Spirit who strengthens you.
> May the heavenly host sustain you
> and the company of heaven enfold you.
> In communion with all the faithful,
> may you dwell this day in peace.
>
> (*A New Zealand Prayer Book/*
> *He Karakia Mihinare o Aotearoa*)

Engage with regrets and forgiveness

I sometimes offer a ritual around forgiveness and regrets; as Howell writes, 'Rarely are there no "if onlys" following a death' (1993, pp. 18–19). Speck too notes this tendency to speculate:

> The bereaved will often say, 'If only . . .' and any ambivalent feelings concerning the deceased will often lead to exaggerated thoughts and actions. A parent of a child who was killed in a road accident said afterwards, 'If only I had made him wait while I brushed his hair he wouldn't have ended up beneath a car.' (Speck, 1978, p. 9)

I provide a wooden box with a hinged lid and small pieces of paper and pens. I then invite parents and family members to engage with any regrets they might have, things they may want to symbolically ask forgiveness for, or memories they may want to leave behind. I then invite them to come up and write them down in full or in their own code, open the box, place the paper inside and symbolically close the lid. I assure them the papers will be confidentially destroyed afterwards. If doing this in a group, I would have a positive activity available at the same time, such as lighting a candle to signify happy memories, so people were not prevented from engaging with regrets by fear of what others might think.

Another aspect of this activity is the potential to begin to engage with anger. I do not major on this in my explanation, but it is a part of the connection and release I hope to facilitate. Staudacher suggests that 'The direction in which your anger is focused will vary depending on your situation, your personality and even your gender. You may be angry at God and religion, the unfairness of "the world", other people, yourself, or even the deceased' (1987, p. 12). Identifying who you are angry with, and why, is important in the grief journey as anger that is not dealt with can cause problems in the future as well as the present. I may also use a confession and absolution if this is appropriate.

Encourage activities

Against the so-called British reserve, I have found that responsive activities with families often generate a fruitful and grateful response. Here are two types of activity that I have found work very well.

Candles

Candles provide an almost universally positive symbol for families to embrace. At BCH we have had personalized candle-holders made and we use these for baptisms, our memorial service and a weekly service in chapel. This is a prayer which may be helpful:

> 'Five candles'
> As we light these five candles in honour of you, we light one for our grief, one for our courage, one for our memories, one for our love, and one for our hope.
>
> This candle represents our grief. The pain of losing you is intense. It reminds us of the depth of our love for you.
>
> This candle represents our courage – to confront our sorrow, to comfort each other, and to change our lives.
>
> This candle is in your memory – the times we laughed, the times we cried, the times we were angry with each other, the silly things you did, and the caring and joy you gave us.

This candle is the light of love. Day by day we cherish the special place in our hearts that will always be reserved for you. We thank you for the gift your living brought to each of us.

And this candle is the light of hope. It reminds us of love and memories of you that are ours forever. May the glow of the flame be our source of hopefulness now and forever.

We love you. (Williams and Sims, 1996, p. 43)

Confetti

There are three things I always have in my bag: a copy of 'Footprints' (see p. 131), a copy of Psalm 23 and confetti. Why confetti? This may seem like a strange medium but let me explain how we use it. I was invited to do an end-of-life baptism for a young person from a large family; there were to be about ten children plus 20 adults present at the bedside service. Being a habitual theological reflector, I had been buying and saving things I thought might be of use in my pastoral work, and in this collection I found some padded gold heart confetti and took it with me. During the service I placed the gold hearts on an engraved plate, put it on the bed and invited the children to come and place a heart on their sibling, cousin or friend. It was at this point that the adults almost pushed the children out of the way in their rush to place the hearts around the teenager and take some for themselves. It did not take me long to realize I was on to something and I frequently offer something similar when I do baptisms or blessings.

Issues in rituals

Should children attend the funeral of their sibling or friend?

It depends on the age and maturity of the child, and usually the family do have an idea of what they want to do. It can be helpful, certainly, for older children, but if a child is attending who is still young enough to need looking after then someone apart from the parents may need to be involved, otherwise there is a danger of the parent not being able to participate in the funeral. Lauren's mum, Michelle, writes

---

We allowed Connor to see Lauren in the Chapel of Rest the day before the funeral and he came to the funeral, as he had asked to do both. He was only five and a half, but I worried that his fear of the unknown would be worse than actually seeing the reality. Five years on and I am glad we made that decision as he had his chance to say goodbye.

Follow-up opportunities

As a hospital chaplain I always try to make contact with a local minister, whether or not the family has a church connection, as I know I cannot offer the ongoing care that may be needed. Thus, from a church perspective, do make connections with the hospital or hospice and find out what they have done and what you may be able to offer. One of the issues local ministers will have is when a sick child has had an emergency baptism, has got better and has gone home. The family may still want the big event at their local church and desire the child to be baptized again. My suggestion is that the local church offers the family a thanksgiving service and provides a ceremony that has many of the components of a baptism, such as godparents. Our experience has been that many families really appreciate this, and it gives both the child and the family a connectedness back to their local community.

Sometimes it can feel to families as if care stops after the funeral. Care needs to go beyond this. Some may appreciate continuing visits, others the opportunity to attend memorial services. Needs differ, but it can be important to try and ascertain if there is a role for the Church's ministry on an ongoing basis.

End-of-life baptisms

Emergency baptisms

Many of the call-outs for the Christian chaplain in a children's hospital will be to do an emergency baptism. The family will have been told that there is nothing more that can be done for the child and that he or she will shortly die or treatment will be withdrawn. Within the care pathway, the nurse will then offer the services of a chaplain and suggest that the family may perhaps like a blessing or baptism.

At this point I think the reason a family might want a baptism changes from the normal reason found in many of our traditions. I have a hypothesis that families want their children to be baptized before they die to ensure as far as possible that the child will go to heaven. In emergency baptism I will use many of the resources I have advocated above. I do not necessarily do a full service, but for a child to have a valid baptism that is recordable in the book and worthy of a certificate, the following is used: 'X, I baptize you in the name of the Father, and of the Son, and of the Holy Spirit.' What is surprising to many nurses we work with is that if they are baptized themselves they can baptize the child and it will be valid.

Baptisms are a core part of the services provided by hospital chaplains. My colleague Kathryn Darby recounts this story, which demonstrates some of the complexities of emergency baptisms.

Within church ministry, often several visits are made with a family preparing for the baptism of their child. Classes might be arranged for adults considering baptism and confirmation. Within a hospital emergency setting, time for careful consideration and preparation is rarely afforded. One example lives with me. I was called to the bedside of a child on ICU who was known to the chaplaincy, Jake, a beautiful boy, less than two years old. His parents were a young couple. Jake had a heart condition which meant that he had spent a long extended time in hospital. His recent turn for the worse meant that the family were both clinging on to hope and also beginning to imagine the unimaginable: that Jake might die. They requested baptism for their son. Their commitment in coming to the hospital and persevering through the bleakest of trials moved me very much. In Catherine, Jake's mum, I witnessed a calm and steady determination and love for her child. When the request was made for baptism, I was ready and glad to respond to their need. Although they had an affiliation with their local church, it was appropriate to proceed with baptism at this juncture when the couple were suddenly at risk of losing Jake.

What I was less prepared for was Catherine's question, as I set out the small portable font and laid out my things, 'Can I be baptized too?' In that suspended moment, I decided in a flash that it was not pastorally sensitive or necessary to explore any more fully the matter of what baptism meant to her, or to hesitate. She knew instinctively, I believe, the significance of the opportunity before her, to be with her son in his baptism from death to life. And I sensed that her faith was pure and simple. The situation had the flavour of Philip's meeting with the Ethiopian eunuch: 'Look, here is water. What is to prevent me from being baptized?' (Acts 8.26–40). Seeing the opportunity and the faith of the eunuch, Philip stops the chariot, the man is baptized and Philip is swept off to another engagement. 'Here is a font,' Jake's mother seemed to say. 'What is to prevent me from being baptized?' That moment illustrates for me the nature of God's grace, which the baptism rite most essentially signals and announces. It was my deepest honour to perform the service.

Baptism for a dead child?

Fortunately, for most in local church ministry this is not going to be a frequent request. Each Christian tradition has its own theological stance on this, but I want to explore what might be going on when this is asked for. For some families, I am sure it is as above: they are afraid God won't let their child into heaven. Alongside this, I think there is some concern around the child having a recognized name. My response to this request is an example of the integrity–expediency tension. I very gently explain that I cannot do a baptism but I can offer a naming ceremony, and I do all but a baptism service except I say 'I name this child' and use oil instead of water. With many of the families I do this for, I don't think they realize there is any difference, and I do not correct them.

Non-religious rituals and resources

We had a situation which is happening more and more: 'We would like you to do X's funeral, but we don't want it to be religious.' One of our team, Nick Ball, did the funeral and these are his reflections on it:

It may mean that a lot of theology and theodicy isn't wanted, it may be that non-religious songs are wanted rather than hymns. It may be that few if any prayers are wanted. Often people are very unsure of what they believe. Sometimes the use of familiar words and phrases can give 'the right feel' to the service, even a sense of 'doing things properly', but for other people it is important to avoid what can be regarded as empty words and phrases that don't actually engage with them or that seem to treat their grief lightly. One family for whom I took their child's funeral asked for me because I had been a real support to them on their journey without ever pushing religion. However, the mother did want to talk about her child's eternal destiny as we approached the end of the little girl's life. The service that I took consisted entirely of tributes and music, and I shared some thoughts about how hard it was to understand what had happened. Only the committal service was 'religious'.

I was asked to do an end-of-life blessing for a family who were not particularly religious. I used the heart confetti and 'Footprints' as a prayer for the family. I also seek out liturgies that are spiritual rather than exclusively religious, such as this:

> Our pain in letting go is the honouring of the love
> which began in us
> and which is now carried forth
> into all the winds of the skies and the tides of the seas,
> into the shining of the sun and the gentle light of the moon
> travelling with the tiny life of X
> in whatever form [he or she] now exists.
>
> (McRae-McMahon 2004)

One of the opportunities that we have developed in recent years is a picnic and walk at the National Memorial Arboretum. It is not a religious event although it was initiated by the chaplaincy. We have a BCH riverside walk, and there is a 'Wind in the Willows' area where families can buy a tree and plaque to remember their child. It is an opportunity for pastoral, spiritual and religious care, which is offered according to the needs of the families.

Memorial services

When I go and talk about my work at local churches I regularly have people coming up to me and sharing their own loss. Sometimes this can be from fifty or more years ago, but the memory is still alive and they value the opportunity of retelling the story. It may be that some want to come year upon year to remember, to acknowledge their child and their loss. One of the people who shared their story said how their child was still part of the family and grandchildren knew about her and asked about her.

Like many hospitals and churches, BCH offers an annual memorial service. This is a parent's reflection:

We have never revisited the children's hospital after Dylan's death, simply because the memories are too painful; however, we do attend the memorial service offered by the hospital. It provides an open place for tears to flow freely. I find the mention of your child's name endearing and the service is a great honour to your child's life. I do have a faith. I believe that Dylan has eternal life. I wrestled with my religion in the early days but now I find comfort from it. Praying and lighting a candle are an important part of my ritual in remembering Dylan's life.

Our principles in designing the memorial service are to make it personal, to read out the names of the children (this seems to be universally appreciated) and to make it creative, responsive and participative, with parents bringing up personalized candles, prayer leaves, etc. We aim for variety by including well-known and personal poems, solos, a choir, hymns and a short accessible talk.

A key issue for us is how long you keep inviting people back. We invite families who have been bereaved in the past year up until three months before the service; we have this cut-off time, at the guidance of our bereavement team, so that the grief is not so raw and the family can come to remember and honour their child without the grief being so all-consuming. We also invite those who have attended in previous years. Recently we have done this by putting next year's dates on the current year's order of service, as the numbers were growing so quickly that personal invitations were becoming too large an administrative job (to date, BCH Chaplaincy only has a volunteer secretary, who is a star). The outline of our service can be found in Appendix 5.

The annual memorial service does not necessarily fulfil the anniversary objective, but it does give the family the opportunity to remember their child. This can be a wonderful opportunity for the Church to reach out to families with whom it may have had a fleeting but significant contact. Some churches have a book of remembrance where people can have an inscription, and some families appreciate coming and seeing this on the anniversary of a death.

I really like the concept of sacred places on earth being thin places, where the felt distance between earth and heaven is very small. My desire is that our hospital chapel should be one of these, and sometimes families tell me that when they go in they can sense God in this place. I wonder if one aspect of this is that the years of prayers that have gone up with tears and pleading have shed their fragrance. Making a space available for people to spend some time in quiet reflection might be something for churches to consider, particularly if there is the opportunity to light candles or participate in some other ritual.

Be mindful of how others interpret things

During a recent phone call from a mother who lost one of her twins in 2003, a concern was shared on behalf of the remaining twin, now approaching six years of age. Kathryn explains the issue:

Last year, while Mum was telling the events of Easter to the remaining twin, a son, together with another sibling, the twin became very upset and asked why his sister couldn't be raised from the dead like Jesus. Naturally, Mum was so surprised by this question from a then five-year-old. It made her think, and realize that while she was coping with the bereavement and grieving process, this little one wasn't. She had been given a book from someone in the hospital to read to her son, but this only made him more upset. This had been approximately six weeks ago. (I suggested she might leave it a little while and perhaps read it again in a few weeks' time, as on that occasion he would probably remember the story and be less upset by it.) The purpose of the phone call was to ask if she and her son could be invited along to the memorial service so that he could see he was not alone to have a sister die. Seeing others, children particularly, he might be able to talk to them about their brothers and sisters who had died and feel more able to cope with his own grief.

Some general tips

- Don't worry about using an idea more than once, but do personalize each service. I use 'Footprints' at most of the rituals I do as I find it connects to many stages of grief. Many appreciate lighting a candle.
- Don't worry about showing your own grief, but don't do it in a way that detracts from what you are doing and makes you the focus of attention. If you are vulnerable in certain areas it can be helpful to share the leading with someone else who can take over if you do break down.
- Give the family things to take away. I often try and include this as part of the rituals I lead. I have already mentioned forget-me-nots, but it may also be a heart or a candle or something that particularly signifies that child.
- Use phrases like 'as a Christian, I believe . . .'
- For funerals, discuss a double slot at the crematorium or cemetery when you get the request, or negotiate with the family if you are planning the funeral with them before they go to the funeral director. Some families may not want a long service but if there are several people who want to give tributes, for example, then just over 20 minutes is not long.

For reflection

- Do you find children's funerals more difficult? If so, why? What measures can you put in place to address your concerns?
- Thinking of funeral services you have been to, what has been helpful? Unhelpful?
- How might this help you plan funerals for children and young people?
- What resources do you take with you when going to discuss a child's funeral? What else might be helpful?
- Do any of the ideas and suggestions in this chapter resonate with you? How might they impact your practice?
- Are there any memorial activities or events that might be a helpful addition to what you currently offer?

Conclusion

> Grieving is hard work, exhausting in fact, and any supporting measure is greatly welcomed by the bereaved. (Dylan's family)

As we come to the end of the book I want to encourage reflection on what sort of minister and carer we are or want to be to those experiencing the sickness, dying or death of a child. Each of us needs to decide what it is we have, and what we want to and can give – time, listening ears, our full attention, our vulnerability, our powerlessness . . . – remembering that often God equips and empowers us one moment at a time. I have sought to crystallize my thinking in this charter.

Charter for palliative and bereavement care

I will commit myself to the following:

1 I will take time to listen to the story and experience of the family. I will seek to build a relationship of mutual trust. I will ask, not assume, and will seek permission. I will honour and respect. I will not abuse my power.
2 I will be confident in and cultivate who I am, to and around children and their families, remembering that this is more important than what I say. The type of person I want to be is gracious, generous, patient, compassionate, kind, courageous, honest, helpful, empowering, being compassionate first and last. I will follow prompts, be bold yet gentle, minister with intentional availability and vulnerability. I will draw upon God's gifts of discernment and wisdom in how to respond.
3 I will be a minister of presence, comfort, peace, hope, redemption, forgiveness, resurrection and mystery.
4 I will befriend death and be more comfortable around dying children and bereaved families, being willing to name the elephant in the room. I will be a channel of appropriate hope.
5 I will have a care plan to keep in touch with the family and will not avoid them. I will not be debilitated by a fear of saying the wrong thing. I will create space and give permission for questions, doubts and concerns. I will not be formulaic in caring, realizing that families will differ in how they process their anticipated or realized loss, but also that there are patterns in grieving.
6 I will be creative in my care, liturgy and rituals.

7 I will offer or facilitate practical help such as shopping, cooking, attending appointments, registering the death, etc.
8 I will be aware of the tension between pastoral and theological integrity and expediency. Sometimes being pastorally and theologically expedient is good theology and pastoral care.
9 I will fight the natural tendency to make sense of what has happened right this minute.
10 I will offer support and, if needed, give permission that a new normal life is achievable and acceptable.
11 I will look after myself and value my role as part of a multidisciplinary team. I will be reflective, self-aware, honest with myself, mindful of triggers and willing to refer when necessary.
12 I will relax. There is nothing I might say that is worse than what has already happened.

Best practice

Of all the things that I have covered in this book, these are the core elements of best practice that I believe anyone working in this context needs to be aware of:

- Be mindful of meeting different types of care: religious, spiritual, pastoral and cultural.
- Don't feel you always have to speak or have the answers. Words are a blunt instrument. And sometimes all we have is 'I am so sorry for your news, for your loss.'
- It is up to the family to make sense of their pain. It is not the role of the professional to do it for them. Fight the natural tendency to make complete sense of the situation. Don't redeem too quickly.
- Be both pro- and reactive in your care.
- Speak to and encourage others to talk to the child, regardless of the level of consciousness. Use the child's name and be aware of his or her humanity.
- Be inclusive of all members of the family. Include those who may be disenfranchised and try to engage with all ages.
- Don't take the expressed emotions of the family personally or permanently.
- Don't get drawn into protecting or defending the reputation of God. Where appropriate, reframe the question to look at what God is like.
- Pray with wisdom and discernment, and be aware that what you can always pray for is God's peace, strength and perspective for the children and the families.

- Seek to act ethically and with integrity, and be willing to help families explore ethical issues that may be involved in their situation.
- Be aware of the procedures leading up to, at and after death, including understanding care pathways, so that you can give the family appropriate support.

Along with these best-practice elements there are some key things to remember:

- Bereavement is only one type of loss that families may be going through.
- Grief is usually a spiral, not linear – a whirlpool is complex.
- Families do become experts in caring for their child, and we can learn from them.
- Our pastoral care reveals our theological hands.
- Individual family members will respond in different ways and heal at different rates. Loss will often be felt way beyond the family.
- Dead children do not trump everything, although it is an immense tragedy to lose a child.
- It is important to articulate our own values. Mine are that the best interests of the child – the needs of the child – should always be at the centre of the care within the family.
- Be honest, even when it's painful.
- Be present: we must make ourselves sacrificially available.
- Be an agent of peace and hope.

Top tips from families

We asked families to tell us their top tips for professionals seeking to work in palliative and bereavement care. This is what they recommended:

1 Listen to our stories, be there for the long haul and continue to talk about our child.
2 Offer help with the practical things of life like shopping or picking up children from school or cooking a meal, and just drop in and visit to help us avoid feeling isolated.
3 It helps to be reassured that our child is no longer in pain because as a mother I always want what is best for my child. It helps to know that God understands how we feel.
4 Our memories are really important for us to hang on to. Where possible facilitate the creation of memories through rituals. Be willing to keep listening to our memories.

5 It can be really helpful to come to memorial services, both for us as families but also for our or our child's friends, as it enables us to continue to show our love for our child. Having our child's name in a remembrance book is a comfort too.

If there was one word to sum up everything else it is this – listen.

As the years go on, please don't forget us. Even if you've not seen our faces for a while, our lives will never be the same again. There will always be someone missing and there will always be something special about you who cared. (Tabea's family)

Appendix 1
Useful contacts and resources

Helpline numbers for bereaved parents

Child Bereavement Charity: confidential support and information service for bereaved children and families, open 9–5 Monday to Friday with answerphone at other times: 01494 568900. <www.childbereavement.org.uk>.

The Child Death Helpline: for anyone affected by the death of a child of any age, from pre-birth to adult, under any circumstances, however recently or long ago. Calls are answered by bereaved parents and an interpreting service is available. Open Monday to Friday 10–1, Tuesday and Wednesday 1–4 and every evening 7–10: 0800 282 986 (freephone). <www.childdeathhelpline.org.uk>.

The Compassionate Friends: dedicated to the support and care of those who have suffered the death of a child. Calls are answered by bereaved parents who will listen and can also put you in touch with your nearest group in the UK and provide information and leaflets. The helpline is open every day of the year and also offers support and information to those supporting bereaved families. Open 10–4 and 7–10: 0845 123 2304. <www.tcf.org.uk>.

Supportline: confidential emotional support for children, young people or adults: 01708 765200. <www.supportline.org.uk>.

Other organizations

ACT (Association for Children's Palliative Care): palliative care focus, 0845 108 2201. <www.act.org.uk>.

Bereavement Advice Centre: information and advice about practical issues following a death, 0800 634 9494. <www.bereavementadvice.org>.

Bereavement UK: information about death, dying, funerals, etc. <www.bereavement.co.uk>.

Beyond the Horizon: Birmingham-based help for bereaved children and young people: 0121 430 7529. <www.beyondthehorizon.org.uk>.

Bliss: special care baby charity, 0500 618140. <www.bliss.org.uk>.

Children's Hospices UK: 0117 989 7820. <www.childhospice.org.uk>.

CLIC Sargent: for children and young people with cancer: 0800 197 0068. <www.clicsargent.org.uk>.

Contact a Family: advice, information and support for those whose child has a disability: 0808 808 3555. <www.cafamily.org.uk>.

Cruse: bereavement care: 0844 477 9400. <www.crusebereavementcare.org.uk>. RD4U is the children and young people's branch: 0808 808 1677. <www.rd4u.org.uk>.

Freshwinds: Birmingham-based charity offering complementary therapies. <www.freshwinds.org.uk>.

FSID (Foundation for the Study of Infant Deaths): cot death support: 0808 802 6868. <www.sids.org.uk>.

Grandparents' Association: 0845 434 9585. <www.grandparents-association.org.uk>.

Grief Encounter: helping siblings: 020 8446 7452. <www.griefencounter.com>.

Inquest: free advice on contentious deaths. <www.inquest.org.uk>.

Just Giving: can personalize a site to raise money for a charity of your choice. <www.justgiving.com>.

Much Loved: for creating memorials. <www.muchloved.com/g_home.aspx>.

PAPYRUS (Prevention of Young Suicide): 0800 068 4141. <www.papyrus-uk.org>.

RoadPeace: for road accident victims and their families: 0845 4500 355. <www.roadpeace.org>.

SAMM (Support after Murder and Manslaughter): 0845 872 3440. <www.samm.org.uk>.

SANDS (Stillbirth and Neonatal Death Society): 020 7436 5881. <www.uk-sands.org>.

SOBS (Survivors of Bereavement by Suicide): 0844 561 6855. <www.uk-sobs.org.uk>.

Winston's Wish: childhood bereavement charity, 0845 203 0405. <www.winstonswish.org.uk>.

Books

Resources produced by ACT

ACT, 2004. *Framework for the Development of an Integrated Multi-agency Care Pathway for Children with Life-limiting Conditions*. London, ACT.

ACT, 2007. *The ACT Transition Care Pathway: A framework for the development of integrated multi-agency care pathways for young people with life-threatening and life-limiting conditions*. Bristol, ACT.

ACT, 2009. *A Family Companion to the ACT Care Pathway for Children with Life-limiting and Life-threatening Conditions*. Bristol, ACT.

ACT, 2009. *A Guide to the Development of Children's Palliative Care Services*, 3rd edition. Bristol, ACT.

ACT, 2009. *A Neonatal Pathway for Babies with Palliative Care Needs*. Bristol, ACT.

Helpful resources produced by CBC

Farewell My Child: a range of families' stories, from those whose baby died at birth to those who have experienced the death of adult children; and from those where the death was sudden to those where the death was anticipated.

I Miss My Sister: the words and illustrations help to guide a child through the different emotions often encountered following the death of a sibling.

My Brother and Me: the simple story deals with the issues surrounding a sibling's serious illness and stays in hospital, and how his brother copes with different emotions and feelings.

Remembering: part book, part scrapbook, this was created to help keep a child's memories alive after the loss of someone special and to give children a place to return to whenever they wish.

Someone I Know Has Died: an activity book with interactive features, written for bereaved children to help them understand what it means when someone dies and to help them explore their thoughts and feelings with an adult. This book is designed for early years children.

All the above are available from CBC (contact details on p. 153).

Other helpful publications

Children's Cancer and Leukaemia Group (CCLG), 2007. *Bereavement: Where to go for help. A guide for families and professionals when a child or young person has died from cancer.* Available as a download from <www.cclg.org.uk>.

Dignity Caring Funeral Services, 2010. *A Child's Questions about Death.* Available as a download from <www.dignityfunerals.co.uk>.

Goldman, A., Hain, R. and Liben, S. (eds), 2006. *Oxford Textbook of Palliative Care for Children.* Oxford, Oxford University Press.

Tonkin, Lois, 2008. *In Our Own Words: Parents talk about life after their child has died.* CLIC Sargent. Available as a download from <www.clicsargent.org.uk>.

Gift books

Allen, G., Rusaw, R., Stuecher, D. and Williams, P. S. (eds), 2004. *When I'm Coping with Loss.* Cincinnati, Standard Publishing.

Baker, K., 2009. *Empty Arms.* Darlington, E.P. Books.

Mayfield, S., 2008. *Living with Bereavement.* Oxford, Lion.

Peterson, E. H., 2005. *A Message of Comfort and Hope.* Nashville, J. Countryman.

Rundle, E., 2001. *You're Never Alone.* Stowmarket, Kevin Mayhew.

Scripture Union, 2007. *Wise Traveller.* Bletchley, Scripture Union.

Books to help you work with individuals and groups with exercises, worksheets, etc.

Auz, M. M. and Andrews, M. L., 2002. *Handbook for Those Who Grieve.* Chicago, Loyola Press.

Cowlishaw, S. and Gale, C., 1993. *When My Little Sister Died.* Dublin, Merlin Publishing.

Durant, A., 2004. *Always and Forever.* London, Corgi Children's Press.

Dyregrov, A., 1991. *Grief in Children.* London, Jessica Kingsley.

Merrington, B., 2008. *When Someone Dies.* Stowmarket, Kevin Mayhew.

Mood, P. and Whittaker, L., 2001. *Finding a Way Through When Someone Close Has Died.* London, Jessica Kingsley.

Mundy, M., 2004. *Sad isn't Bad: A good grief guidebook for kids dealing with loss.* St Meinrad, Abbey Press.

Perkins, J., 2007. *How to Help a Child Cope with Grief.* Slough, Foulsham.
Smith, H. I., 2002. *Finding Your Way to Say Goodbye.* Notre Dame, Indiana, Ave Maria Press.
Stickney, D., 2004. *Waterbugs and Dragonflies.* London, Geoffrey Chapman.
Ward, B., 1992. *Good Grief: Exploring feelings, loss and death with over 11s and adults.* Uxbridge, Good Grief.

Appendix 2
Care pathways

Stages in a palliative care pathway

1 *Breaking news* Every family should receive the disclosure of their child's prognosis in a face-to-face discussion in privacy and should be treated with respect, honesty and sensitivity. Information should be provided for both the child and the family in language that they can understand.
2 *Discharge home* Every child and family diagnosed in the hospital setting should have an agreed transfer plan involving the hospital, community services and the family. They should be provided with the resources they require before leaving hospital.
3 *Needs assessment* Every family should receive a multi-agency assessment of their needs as soon as possible after diagnosis or recognition, and should have their needs reviewed at appropriate intervals.
4 *Care planning* Every child and family should have a multi-agency care plan agreed with them for the delivery of co-ordinated care and support to meet their individual needs. A keyworker to assist with this should be identified and agreed with the family.
5 *End of life* Every child and family should be helped to decide on an end-of-life plan and should be provided with the care and support to achieve this as closely as possible.
6 *Post death* Opportunities will be provided for the family to see the child and to access support as appropriate.

Appendix 3
Multi-faith perspectives

The information below should only be used as a rough guide. As with Christianity, there are many different traditions within each world religion. It is important to note that there are some differences between children and adults, and the information here is specifically for children. A good general principle, if you are involved in any discussions with families from other faiths, is that they will appreciate an explanation for what is being asked or required. There is a commonly held reservation of harming the body after death. I am currently launching a project, Red Balloon Resources, to develop resources for bereaved families and healthcare staff training. Please email me on <rbr@bch.nhs.uk> for further details.

Buddhism

Care of the dying, end of life

The family may not wish sedatives to be used. They may wish to wash the child's body.

Provide a place and space of peace and quiet.

Visit from the religious leader

Call a monk to facilitate peace and quiet for meditation.

Organ donation

No religious preference as norm.

Postmortem

No religious preference as norm.

Funeral

Cremation is preferred but will depend on tradition.

Beliefs about suffering

Suffering is universal and is eased by not being selfish.

Belief about the afterlife

Buddhists believe in rebirth.

Hinduism

Care of the dying, end of life

Any jewellery and sacred threads should not be removed.

After death, close the child's eyes and straighten the body. The family may wish the body to be placed on the floor. They may wish to wash the body and wrap it in a white cloth. Holy water may be applied to the lips.

Visit from the religious leader

A priest may be required, reading from the holy books.

Organ donation

No major issues.

Postmortem

No religious preference as norm.

Funeral

The funeral takes place as soon as possible after death. Children under five may be buried; adults are cremated.

Beliefs about suffering

Varied attitudes.

Belief about the afterlife

Hindus believe in rebirth.

Islam

Care of the dying, end of life

Upon imminent death Muslims may wish to recite a certain chapter from the Qur'an around the dying; this is believed to help the departure of the soul. The dying patient may wish to face Mecca (a south-easterly direction in the UK).

Upon death the eyes and mouth are closed, the body is straightened, the head is turned slightly to the right (as the body will be buried with the head facing Mecca) and the body is covered with a clean sheet. Any sacred jewellery should not be removed.

Washing has to be in accordance with the Islamic faith.

Privacy is needed for the family to grieve.

Families may wish to take the child home with them. They will use Muslim undertakers.

Visit from the religious leader

Offer a visit from an imam, but prayers are normally led by the family.

Organ donation

Varied attitudes. It is allowed by Islamic guidance in the UK, but there is concern about the body being harmed and incomplete.

Postmortem

Not keen; this could be very distressing for families as some may believe that the child will feel pain. However, it is allowed if necessary.

Funeral

The funeral takes place as soon as possible after death, preferably within 24 hours, so that the soul can go to rest, and to preserve the aesthetic appearance of the body. Muslims are always buried. Muslims believe in paradise or hell; young children are assured of paradise and can intercede for their parents to enter paradise without judgement. There is no official funeral for a stillborn child, only private prayers.

Beliefs about suffering

Death is seen as the will of God. Muslims believe that the life span of every individual was allocated at the beginning of time. Suffering is to be borne with forbearance, perseverance and acceptance of God's will. Suffering atones for one's sins and raises one's status in the hereafter.

Belief about the afterlife

After death the soul enters the intermediary world and awaits Judgement Day. There is a belief in heaven and hell. Infants enter into the care of the prophet Abraham and have a happy and prosperous time in the intermediary world; they are assured of heaven and are a security and blessing for their family.

Judaism

Care of the dying, end of life

Jews may wish to hear Psalm 23 read and the *Shema*. The body should be handled as little as possible. After death the eyes should be closed, clothing kept as it is and the body covered with a sheet then left untouched for a short time. Enquire about washing the body as the family may wish to do this. Some traditions may require same-gender contact only. There will be Jewish undertakers.

Visit from the religious leader

Offer a visit from a rabbi, but readings are normally led by the family.

Organ donation

Varied attitudes; refer to rabbi.

Postmortem

Varied attitudes; some families will be very much against it. Again, refer to rabbi.

Funeral

The funeral takes place as soon as possible after death and if possible within 24 hours. A 'watcher' sits with the body within some traditions. Jews may prefer burial in a separate cemetery.

Beliefs about suffering

Varied attitudes.

Belief about the afterlife

Jews believe in life after death in heaven or hell. Infants are assured of heaven in most traditions.

Sikhism

Care of the dying, end of life

The family will read from the holy books; there are no priests. Music or prayers may be played. After death close the eyes and straighten the body. The family may wish to wash and dress the body. If the child is a boy past puberty, he will wear a white turban and this should not be removed. The five Ks – the physical symbols worn by Sikhs – should be retained. These are a wooden comb, a steel bracelet, special shorts or underwear, a small sword, an uncut beard and uncut hair, covered by a turban.

Visit from the religious leader

Offer a visit from a guru, but reading can be led by the family.

Organ donation

Varied attitudes, generally acceptable.

Postmortem

No main issues.

Funeral

Sikhs are always cremated and the ashes poured into flowing water. Mourners wear white.

Beliefs about suffering

Varied attitudes.

Belief about the afterlife

Sikhs believe in rebirth.

Appendix 4
End-of-life baptism or blessing

Welcome

Leader: Lord, we welcome you to this bedside. We thank you that you love us and are here with us. You know our joys and share our sorrows. We are gathered here to bless little [child's name].

Reading: Skylark haiku (p. 130)

Thanksgiving

Leader: We thank you, Lord, for the gift of [this child], for the gift of life, even for such a short time. We thank you for the love we have been given and thank you for the love we have been able to give to [him or her].

We remember the times of joy and times of sadness, but most of all we thank you for this gift of life. We all would want it to be longer and would ask that you will be with us and support us in our time of sorrow and distress.

Reading: Psalm 23

Leader: This is God's promise to [this child] and to all of us.

The two greatest gifts, no matter how long we live, are to love and be loved.

All sprinkle heart confetti .

Reading: Romans 8.35–39

Blessing

Bless family members if requested

Baptism

Leader: By the authority given to me, I now welcome you into God's Church.

[Child's name], I baptize you,
in the name of the Father,
and of the Son,
and of the Holy Spirit.
I sign you with the sign of the cross,
a symbol of God's sacrifice and pain.
Receive this sign of the welcome into God's everlasting family,
and know that God will be with you always.

Prayers

Leader: Let us in the silence give thanks to God for the life of this child.
Each moment of the journey with this life is precious to us, O God.
Even as our thankfulness is overwhelmed with grief,
so that our joy is misted in pain,
we give you thanks for this life and all life.

All: Amen.

Leader: We thank you for the love that [this child] gave and the love [he or she] received. Give all here confidence that [he or she] is safe with you, and comfort them with the same love you are now giving to [the child].

May you know God's peace and comfort at this time.

Heavenly Father, you know our thoughts and pain this day. Be with us and bring your comfort. You alone can heal our broken hearts; you alone can wipe away the tears that well up inside us; you alone can give us the peace we need; you alone can strengthen us to carry on. We ask you to be near those whose time of joy has been turned into sadness. Assure them that with you nothing is incomplete, and uphold them with your tender love. Supported by your strength, may our love for one another be deepened by the knowledge of your love for us all.

We remember the good times and the not-so-good times, the times of laughter and of tears. We thank you for the love that was given, received, shared.

Comfort this family with your presence and love. Be with them and help ease their pain and bereavement. Help them to find assurance that nothing with you needs to be wasted. Help us now to have the courage and strength to leave them in your care.

All: Amen.

All say the Lord's Prayer

Farewell

Leader: Heavenly Father,
[the parents or family] have committed [the child's name] to you,
a name to be treasured for ever in their hearts.
You knew [him or her] by name before time began.
Now we commit [him or her] into your ever-caring and gentle love;
we commend [this child] into your loving care.
Enfold [him or her] in your arms of love.
[He or she] will be missed beyond words, Lord God, and never forgotten.
[He or she] brought joy to this family
and to many lives in so short a time;
enfold [him or her] now in eternal life,

in the name of our risen Saviour,
who was born and died and lives and reigns
with you and the Holy Spirit for ever.
To you, gentle Father, we humbly entrust this child,
so precious in your sight.
Take [him or her] into your arms
and welcome [him or her] into your presence,
where there is no sorrow or pain,
but the fullness of peace and joy
with you for ever and ever.

All: Amen.

Leader: [Child's name], go forth from this world:
in the love of God the Father who created you,
in the mercy of Jesus Christ who redeemed you,
in the power of the Holy Spirit who strengthens you.
May the heavenly host sustain you
and the company of heaven enfold you.
In communion with all the faithful,
may you dwell this day in peace.

All sprinkle star confetti

Leader: Those whom we love and lose are no longer where they were before;
they are now wherever we are.
(Partly adapted from <www.cofe.anglican.org/worship/liturgy/commonworship>)

Appendix 5
Sample memorial service outline

Introduction

Song: 'Be still, for the presence of the Lord', sung by the Birmingham Children's Hospital Choir

Leader: Welcome
Opening prayer

Hymn: 'Fleetingly known, yet ever remembered' (p. 136)

Poems (from families)

Reading: Words of encouragement from the Bible, during which we make this response:

Reader: My peace I offer to you.

All: My presence I give to you.

Lighting of the candles, during which the choir will sing 'The Lord's my shepherd'

Leader: You are invited to light the candle you have been given from the Easter Candle and place it on the candle stand. The lighted candle is a reminder of the eternal light in which our loved ones live in the new life God has promised. After the service you will be able to take the candle home.

Poems (from families)

Time for reflection

Song: 'Precious child', sung by Birmingham Children's Hospital Choir

Poems (from families)

The placing of prayer leaves on the prayer tree; a solo is sung

Prayers

Leader: The names of the children will be read and then we will join in the Prayer of Remembrance.

The names are read out

All join in the fourth stanza of 'For the fallen' by Laurence Binyon, <www.firstworldwar.com/poetsandprose/binyon.htm>

All say the Lord's Prayer

Thank you from the Chairman, Birmingham Children's Hospital Foundation Trust

Hymn: 'Lord of all hopefulness'

The blessing

Leader: Each life is indeed a gift, no matter how short, no matter how fragile.
Each life is indeed a gift, to be held in our hearts for ever.

Appendix 6
Sources for liturgical material

Websites on which you can find some helpful liturgical material

<http://bigworldsmallboat.blogspot.com/2008/10/bedside-prayer-for-death-of-child.html>

<www.churchsociety.org/issues_new/liturgy/cw/iss_liturgy_cw_funeral.asp>

<www.cofe.anglican.org/worship/liturgy/commonworship/texts/funeral/funeralofachild.html>

<www.drgareth.info/BirthRite.pdf>

<www.hospitalchaplain.com/htm/l-service-ch-funeral.htm>

<www.jtsma.org.uk/iqs/cpti.5/dbitemid.44/sfa.view/support_events_archive.html>

<http://poeticexpressions.co.uk/grief.htm>

<www.textweek.com/> has resources on all the passages in the Lectionary.

Holy Innocents services

<www.paxchristi.org.uk/Documents/Holy_Innocents.pdf>

<http://wf-f.org/innocents.html>

Sermon

<www.durhamcathedral.co.uk/schedule/sermons/307>

Background reading

<www.cofe.anglican.org/worship/liturgy/commonworship/texts/funeral/theologicalnote.html>

<www.griefsjourney.com>

Resource books

Brind, J. and Wilkinson, T., 2008. *Creative Ideas for Pastoral Liturgy: Funeral, thanksgiving and memorial services*. London, Canterbury Press.

Bush, M. D. (ed.), 2006. *This Incomplete One*. Grand Rapids, Michigan, Eerdmans.

Claye, G., 2006. *Don't Let Them Tell You How to Grieve*. Oxford, OxPen.

Froehlich, M. A., 2000. *An Early Journey Home*. Grand Rapids, Michigan, Discovery House Publishers.

Gordon, T., 2006. *New Journeys Now Begin*. Glasgow, Wild Goose Publications.

Lane Fox, F., 2005. *A Heartbeat Away*. West Wycombe, Child Bereavement Trust.

McRae-McMahon, D., 2004. *Liturgies for Daily Life*. London, SPCK.
O'Keefe Lafser, C., 2002. *Longing for My Child*. Chicago, Loyola Press.
Pott, D., 2007. *Journeying Home*. Chatton, Northumbria Community.
Shawe, M., 1992. *Enduring, Sharing, Loving*. London, Darton, Longman and Todd.
Watson, J. (ed.), 2004. *Poems and Readings for Funerals*. London, Penguin.
Wezeman, P. V. and Wezeman, K. R., 2001. *Finding Your Way When Your Child Dies*. Notre Dame, Indiana, Ave Maria Press.
Whitaker, A., 1984. *All in the End is Harvest*. London, Darton, Longman and Todd.
Wilson, J., 2001. *All Shall Be Well*. Norwich, Canterbury Press.

Music CDs

Fawcett, N., 2005. *Living with Loss*. Kevin Mayhew.
Snell, A., 2003. *The Cry: A requiem for a lost child*. Serious Music.
Taylor-Good, K., undated. *Precious Child*. The Compassionate Friends.
Wetzell, C., 2002. *Joy and Light*. Thomas Nelson.

CDs

Churchill Systems, undated. *Funeral Resources*.

Appendix 7
Adult 'attitude to grief' scale

Read the following statements and decide which response is most appropriate for you. It may help to make a copy, so that you can circle your response.

1 I feel able to face the pain which comes with the loss.
Strongly agree / agree / neither agree nor disagree / disagree / strongly disagree
2 For me, it is difficult to switch off thoughts about the person I have lost.
Strongly agree / agree / neither agree nor disagree / disagree / strongly disagree
3 I feel very aware of my inner strength when faced with grief.
Strongly agree / agree / neither agree nor disagree / disagree / strongly disagree
4 I believe that I must be brave in the face of loss.
Strongly agree / agree / neither agree nor disagree / disagree / strongly disagree
5 I feel that I will always carry the pain of grief with me.
Strongly agree / agree / neither agree nor disagree / disagree / strongly disagree
6 For me, it is important to keep my grief under control.
Strongly agree / agree / neither agree nor disagree / disagree / strongly disagree
7 Life has less meaning for me after this loss.
Strongly agree / agree / neither agree nor disagree / disagree / strongly disagree
8 I think it's best just to get on with life after a loss.
Strongly agree / agree / neither agree nor disagree / disagree / strongly disagree
9 It may not always feel like it but I do believe that I will come through this experience of grief.
Strongly agree / agree / neither agree nor disagree / disagree / strongly disagree

(Machin, 2009, p. 176)

Bibliography

Auz, M. M. and Andrews, M. L., 2002. *Handbook for Those Who Grieve*. Chicago, Loyola Press.

Barritt, P., 2005. *Humanity in Healthcare*. Oxford, Radcliffe.

Bearison, D. J., 2006. *When Treatment Fails*. Oxford, Oxford University Press.

Beauchamp, T. L. and Childress, J. F., 2001. *Principles of Biomedical Ethics*, 5th edition. Oxford, Oxford University Press.

Bowlby, J., 1982. *Loss, Sadness and Depression*. New York, Basic Books.

Brown, E., 2009. *Supporting Bereaved Children: A handbook for primary schools*. London, Help the Hospices.

Brown, E. (ed.), 2002. *The Death of a Child: Care for the child, support for the family*. Birmingham, Acorns Children's Hospice Trust.

Brown, E. with Warr, B., 2007. *Supporting the Child and the Family in Paediatric Palliative Care*. London, Jessica Kingsley.

Brueggemann, W., 1995. *The Psalms: The life of faith*. Minneapolis, Fortress.

Burn, J., 2005. *I'm Still Standing*. Oxford, BRF.

Cobb, M., 2001. *The Dying Soul*. Buckingham, Open University Press.

Cobb, M., 2005. *The Hospital Chaplain's Handbook*. Norwich, Canterbury Press.

Davy, J. and Ellis, S., 2000. *Counselling Skills in Palliative Care*. Buckingham, Open University Press.

de Mello, A., 1985. *One Minute Wisdom*. New York, Doubleday.

Di Ciacco, J. A., 2008. *The Colors of Grief*. London, Jessica Kingsley.

Doehring, C., 2006. *The Practice of Pastoral Care: A postmodern approach*. Louisville, Kentucky, Westminster John Knox.

Duffy, W., 1995. *Children and Bereavement*. London, Church House Publishing.

Dyregrov, A., 1991. *Grief in Children: A handbook for adults*. London, Jessica Kingsley.

Ellington, S. A., 2008. *Risking Truth*. Eugene, Pickwick Publications.

Ewing, S., 2005. *Losing a Baby*. London, Sheldon.

Fiddes, P. S., 2000. *Participating in God*. London, Darton, Longman and Todd.

Fischer, K., 2005. *Imaging Life After Death*. London, SPCK.

Froehlich, M. A., 2000. *An Early Journey Home*. Grand Rapids, Michigan, Discovery House Publishers.

Ghaye, T., 2007. 'Is reflective practice ethical? The case of the reflective portfolio.' *Reflective Practice* 8(2), pp. 151–62.

Gill, R., 2006. *Health Care and Christian Ethics*. Cambridge, Cambridge University Press.

Gittelsohn, R. B., 1975. *Gates of Prayer*. London, Central Conference of American Rabbis and Union of Liberal and Progressive Synagogues.

Goldman, L., 2009. *Great Answers to Difficult Questions about Death*. London, Jessica Kingsley.

Greig, P., 2007. *God on Mute*. Eastbourne, Survivor.

Hamma, R. M., 2004. *In Times of Grieving*. Notre Dame, Indiana, Ave Maria Press.

Hauerwas, S., 1990. *Naming the Silences: God, medicine and the problem of suffering.* Grand Rapids, Michigan, Eerdmans.

Hilborn, D., Thacker, J. and Tidball, D., 2008. *The Atonement Debate*. Grand Rapids, Michigan, Zondervan.

Hoekendijk, J. C., 1967. *The Church Inside Out*. Translated and edited by Isaac C. Rottenberg, L. A. Hoedemaker and Pieter Tijmes. London, SCM Press.

Hope, T., Savulescu, J. and Hendrick, J., 2003. *Medical Ethics and Law: The core curriculum*. London, Churchill Livingstone.

Howell, D., 1993. *The Pain of Parting*. Bramcote, Grove Books.

Huotari, R., 2003. 'A perspective on ethical reflection in multiprofessional care.' *Reflective Practice* 4(2), pp. 121–38.

Hurcombe, L., 2004. *Losing a Child: Explorations in grief.* London, Sheldon Press.

Jackson, E. N., 1978. *The Many Faces of Grief.* London, SCM Press.

Jonsen, A. R., Siegler, M. and Winslade, W. J., 1992. *Clinical Ethics: A practical approach to ethical decisions in clinical medicine*, 3rd edition. New York, McGraw-Hill.

Klass, D., 1996. 'The deceased child in the psychic and social worlds of bereaved parents during the resolution of grief' in D. Klass, P. R. Silverman and S. L. Nickman (eds), *Continuing Bonds: New understandings of grief.* New York, Taylor and Francis.

Knox, I., 2003. *Bereaved*, revised edition. Eastbourne, Kingsway.

Kübler-Ross, E., 2008. *On Death and Dying*. London, Routledge.

Kushner, H. S., 2000. *When Bad Things Happen to Good People*. London, Pan Macmillan.

Lane Fox, F., 2005. *A Heartbeat Away*. West Wycombe, Child Bereavement Trust.

Lapwood, R., 1992. *When Babies Die.* Nottingham, Grove.

Lewis, C. S., 1978. *Surprised by Joy*. Glasgow, Collins.

Longman III, T. and Garland, D. E., 2008. *Psalms: The Expositor's Bible Commentary*. Grand Rapids, Michigan, Zondervan.

Machin, L., 2009. *Working with Loss and Grief.* London, Sage.

McKelvey, R. S., 2006. *When a Child Dies: How pediatric physicians and nurses cope*. Seattle, University of Washington Press.

McRae-McMahon, D., 2004. *Liturgies for Daily Life.* London, SPCK.

Mitton, M. and Parker, R., 1991. *Requiem Healing*. London, Daybreak.

Mood, P. and Whittaker, L., 2001. *Finding a Way Through When Someone Close Has Died*. London, Jessica Kingsley.

Musgrave, B. A. and Bickle, J., 2003. *Partners in Healing: Compassionate visitors for people burdened by illness, grief and loss – a handbook*. Mahwah, Paulist Press.

Narayanasamy, A., 2001. *Spiritual Care: A practical guide for nurses and healthcare practitioners*. London, Quay Books.

Nouwen, H. J. M., 1994. *The Wounded Healer*. London, Darton, Longman and Todd.

O'Connor, J., 2004. *Children and Grief.* Grand Rapids, Michigan, Revell.
O'Shea, J., 2008. *When a Child Dies: Footsteps of a grieving family.* Dublin, Veritas.
Owen, D. M., 2008. *Living through Bereavement.* London, SPCK.
Power, P. D. and Orio, A. D., 2003. *The Resilient Family.* Notre Dame, Indiana, Sorin Books.
Robinson, J., 2005. *Teddy Robinson Stories.* London, Kingfisher.
Skeats, T., 2008. 'Grandparent or munmy: supportive, supported or sidelined?' Unpublished dissertation, University of Birmingham via Sherwood Psychotherapy Training Institute.
Speck, P., 1978. *Loss and Grief in Medicine.* London, Baillière Tindall.
Staudacher, C., 1987. *Beyond Grief.* London, Souvenir Press.
Stillwell, E., 2004. *The Death of a Child: Reflections for grieving parents.* Chicago, ACTA Publications.
Swinton, J., 2007. *Raging with Compassion.* Grand Rapids, Michigan, Eerdmans.
Warrington, K., 2005. *Healing and Suffering.* Carlisle, Paternoster.
Watson, J. (ed.), 2004. *Poems and Readings for Funerals.* London, Penguin.
Weems, A., 1995. *Psalms of Lament.* Louisville, Kentucky, Westminster John Knox.
Wezeman, P. V. and Wezeman, K. R., 2001. *Finding Your Way When Your Child Dies.* Notre Dame, Indiana, Ave Maria Press.
Williams, S. L. and Sims, D., 1996. *Holiday Help: A guide for holidays and special days.* Louisville, Kentucky, Accord Aftercare Services.
Wilson, J. with McCreary, A., 2001. *All Shall Be Well.* Norwich, Canterbury Press.
Wilson, R., 1993. 'Bereavement care – the role of the paediatrician.' *Current Paediatrics* 3(2), pp. 86–91.
Woodward, J., 2005. *Befriending Death.* London, SPCK.
Wright, T., 2007. *Surprised by Hope.* London, SPCK.
Yancey, P., 1990. *Where Is God When It Hurts?* Grand Rapids, Michigan, Zondervan.
Young, W. P., 2007. *The Shack.* London, Hodder.

Index of biblical references

OLD TESTAMENT

Exodus
1.15–22 28
12.29 28

1 Samuel
17.42 32

2 Samuel
12.1–31 28, 29

1 Kings
17.1–24 28
17.17–24 36

2 Kings
4.1–44 28
4.17–37 36

Job
whole book 30

Psalms
23 135
139 32

Ecclesiastes
3.2–3 31

Isaiah
61.1 42
61.2 42

NEW TESTAMENT

Matthew
2.16–18 28
9.18–25 36
19.13–15 136

Luke
7.11–15 36
23.43 34

John
13.34 42
15.12, 17 42

Acts
8. 26–40 144
9.36–42 36
20.7–12 36

Romans
5.3 32
8.35 33
12.10 42
15.7 42

1 Corinthians
12.25 42

Galatians
6.2 42

Ephesians
4.32 42

1 Thessalonians
4.18 42
5.15 42

Hebrews
10.24 42

James
1.2–4 32
5.16 42

1 Peter
1.6 32
1.17 72
1.22 42
4.9, 10 42

Revelation
21.4 34

Index of names and subjects

abandonment 21
adolescence 84
adult 'attitude to grief' scale 168
advocate 52
aloneness 10
altruism 55
anniversaries 80
answers 46, 53
anxiety 109, 110
ashes 106
assessment 104
Association for Children's Palliative Care (ACT) 111, 153
attachment 65
autonomy 121
Auz, M. M. and Andrews, M. L. 88
availability 43, 60, 119, 149
awkward, feeling 63

bad news 45; breaking 63, 157
baptism 45, 143, 162; for a dead child 144; emergency 117, 143
Barritt, P. 143
Beauchamp, T. L. and Childress, J. F. 121
bedwetting 65
beneficence 121
bereavement: journey 16; story 76
Bereavement Advice Centre 153
bereavement counsellor 98
Bereavement UK 153
best interests 68, 121
Beyond the Horizon 113, 153
biblical truth 39
birthdays 80, 81
blame 28, 30, 49
blessing 68
Bliss 153
boundaries 9, 46, 56
boys 84
Brown, E. with Warr, B. 10, 69
Buddhism 158
burial 50, 106
Burn, J. 9, 67
cancer 92, 93, 97
candles 141
car accident 49
care: bereavement 8, 19; cultural 6; end-of-life 7, 8, 15; palliative 7, 8, 49; pastoral 3, 4; pathways 157; planning 157; religious 3, 5; spiritual 3, 4
caring for carers 56
'Celebrating brief lives' 132
cemetery 81
challenge 54, 104
charter for palliative and bereavement care 149
Child Bereavement Charity (CBC) 83, 112, 153
Child Death Helpline 112, 153
Children's Hospices UK 153
Christmas 80, 81, 86
churches, equipping 16
CLIC Sargent 153
Clinical Ethics Committee 119
coffin 105
collaborative discussions 95
colluding 53
comfort 22, 39, 42, 117, 138, 149
community healthcare 18
compassion 25, 38, 42, 44, 53, 55, 119, 121, 149; fatigue 56
Compassionate Friends, The 153
complementary therapies, integrating 111
complementary therapist 110, 111
complicity 53
condolence book 108
confidentiality 120
conflict 53
consent 119
consequences 116, 118
consequentialism 116
constraints 52
Contact a Family 153
control 47, 93

coroner 104, 105
counselling 103, 113, 114
courageous 139, 149
covenant 34
creation 26
creativity 135, 149
cremation 50, 106
cross, the 34
Cruse 153
crying, excessive 65
cultural care 6; expectations 117; norms 8
cure 35

death: befriending 47, 149; children's understanding of 64; good 111; imminent 8, 17, 48, 91, 92, 97, 104; welcoming 18
'Death is nothing at all' (Scott Holland) 76, 128
debriefing 56, 58, 108
deferment of power 117
demons 25
deontologicalism 116
dependency 51
depression 104, 109
detachment, emotional and professional 57, 103
diagnosis 9, 10
dignity 101
direct speech 79
discernment 38, 44, 55, 121, 149, 150; discerner 51
discharge home 157
disillusionment 10
distraction 96
donation 95
double grief 84
duty 118
Dyregrov, A. 83–4

elephant in the room 1, 149
empathy 44, 102
empowering 50, 60, 132, 149; disempowering 50
end of life 94; blessing 67, 162; rituals 19, 49, 86
environment 98
equations: healthy 24; unhealthy 24

eternal life 35, 39
ethical dilemmas in healthcare, process for dealing with 122
ethics 49; of care 118; principles 121; professional codes of 98; virtue 121
ethnic norms 8
euthanasia 116
evil 25, 27
expectations 54; cultural 117
extrovert 52

fairness 24, 28
faith community 99
family: care suite 107; disagreement 51; dynamics 48, 125; wishes 106
fault 22
fear 30, 55
Fiddes, P. S. 26
finance 11
'Five candles' 141
'Fleetingly known, yet ever remembered' 136
follow-up opportunities 143
'Footprints' 38, 131
forgiveness 9, 45, 77, 149
Foundation for the Study of Infant Deaths (FSID) 154
free will 25
Freshwinds 154
Froehlich, M. A. 30
fundraising and campaigning 86
funeral 11, 19, 57, 102, 105, 108, 125, 129, 140; children attending 142; directors 97, 98, 105; examples 132

gallows humour 56
games 50
gender issues 84
general practitioner (GP) 99, 102, 104
genetic diagnosis 17
Gethsemane experience 101
Gill, R. 121, 123
girls 84
God allowing suffering 22, 24; and faith 35; as judgement 25; and love 33, 38; as test 25

godparents 143
God's representative 102
goodbye, saying 48, 49, 67, 139, 163
grace 22, 138; gracious 43, 60, 149
grandparents 84, 85
Grandparent's Association 154
grief 44, 99, 108, 109; complicated 16, 17; indulgent 54; liberating 17; minister's own 56, 59; phases of 16; process 13–17, 147; space for 57; substitutes 76; theories of 17; triple 85
Grief Encounter 154
guilt 9, 17, 103

Hauerwas, S. 26
headstone 106
healing 23, 35, 36, 38
heaven and hell 34, 35
Hinduism 159
Holy Spirit 35, 44
honesty 56, 62, 67, 149, 151
hope 22, 25, 35, 39, 69, 95, 96, 149, 151; appropriate 45
hospice 18, 107
hospital-based youth worker 97
hospital play service 96
hostility 48
human rights 120
humanity 26, 57; fall of 25
Hurcombe, L. 49, 76

'I am wearing a pair of shoes' 127
incarnational ministry 43
inequality 10
inquest 104, 154
integrated care pathway 112
integrity 119, 121, 151
interventions 25, 99
introvert 52
Islam 159
isolation 48, 112

journey 23, 42, 75
Judaism 160
Just Giving website 81, 154
justice 34
Kant's categorical imperative 119
Kushner, H. S. 21

lament 127
Lane Fox, F. 15
law 104
letting go 17
Lewis, C. S. 59
listening 44, 53, 93, 149, 151, 152; active 44
'Litany of remembrance' 134
loneliness 9
Lord's Prayer 139
loss 10, 16, 17, 44, 59, 151; accumulated 17
love 24, 31, 33, 38, 42, 119, 138, 139; loving God 25, 26, 30, 39

Machin, L. 52, 168
Macmillan nurses 92, 93
mask 15
meaning 96
Mello, A. de 24
memorial 107, 109; cards 133; service 79, 146, 165
memory 151; board 108; boxes 71
metaphors 12, 43, 56, 59; rollercoaster 12, 15; whirlpool 12, 13, 14
mindfulness 60, 147, 150
minister: own children 57; own faith 102; own skill level 99
minister of presence 149
ministerial ethics 119
miracles 23, 35, 36, 37, 38, 74
miscarriage 8, 10, 32
mortuaries 92, 98
motives 55
Much Loved 154
multidisciplinary team 150
multigenerational 139
multiple medical conditions 97
murder 49
music 136
mystery 96, 149; embracing 39

naming the pain 130
Narayanasamy, A. 2
National Institute for Health and Clinical Excellence (NICE) 122
National Memorial Arboretum 82, 145
needs, assessment of 157
'new normal' 88

night terrors 65
non-judgemental, being 47
non-maleficence 121
normalizing activities 97
Northumbria Community 54, 60
Nouwen, H. J. M. 33

older children 34
organ donation 50, 87, 120
Orio, A. D. 48
over-reliance 51

Paediatric Chaplaincy Network 83
paediatric intensive care consultant 90
paediatric intensive care unit (PICU) 90–2
parents: capacity of 18; separated 86
parish priest 101
pastoral expediency 39, 40, 53, 128, 150
patient advisory and liaison services 52
peace 39, 72, 74, 138, 149, 150, 151
persecutor 50
personal belongings: clothing 105; photographs 109
perspective 150
platitudes 53
play 65, 113
postmortems 97, 98
power 55
Power, P. D. 48
powerlessness 149
practical help, facilitating 150
praxis 44
prayer 25, 122, 135, 138, 145; intercessory 72
praying 23, 25, 35, 37, 42, 72, 122
Prevention of Young Suicide (PAPYRUS) 154
principles 115
providence 28
psychological process 99

quality of life 122
questions: questioning 95; tough 39
reason 25
reassurance, appropriate 103
redemption 25, 39, 149
referral 18, 97, 99, 107; self-referral 97
reflective practitioner 56
refusal of treatment 119
regrets and forgiveness 140
rescuer 50
resilience 98
resource allocation 121
respect 149
responsibility 27; legal 86
rest 9
resurrection 128, 149
resuscitation 91
rights 118
risk-taking behaviour 97
rituals 45, 68; non-religious 145
rollercoaster 12
routines 68

sacred places 147
sacrificial 39, 43, 44, 60
sad 109
SAKE 43
Satan 25
school 78, 102, 108, 114; counsellor 108
self-awareness 47, 52, 58
self-care 56, 58
self-esteem 97, 110
separation anxiety 65
sermon 137
services, leading 138
The Shack 7
shalom 34
shame 17
shock 11, 36, 56
siblings 9, 82, 94, 98, 109, 142
Sikhism 161
silence 52
sin 25, 27
skylark's song 130
sleep, disturbed 65
spiritual: care 3, 4; caregiver 96
spirituality 2
staff, educating 97
Staudacher, C. 125
Stillbirth and Neonatal Death Society (SANDS) 154
strength 39, 72, 150

stress 110
suffering 21, 22, 25, 26, 33, 37, 38; transforming 38
supervision 114
Support after Murder and Manslaughter (SAMM) 154
support: emotional 96, 97, 193; facilitating peer 108; life 37; structure 18, 49, 56, 82, 89
Survivors of Bereavement by Suicide (SOBS) 154
Swinton, J. 27
symptom control 93

telling others 9
temptation 40, 53, 54, 61
tension 38, 39
terminal illness 8, 9, 10
testing 32
thanksgiving 162; service 143
theodicy 145
theological: integrity 39, 40, 53, 150; reflections 33, 34
therapeutic play 96
time to die 31
transactional analysis 50
transcendence 96
transplants 36, 94
treatment: refusal of 119; withholding or withdrawing 120
trials 32
triggers 61
trust 67

uncertainty 95
unexpected 17, 47, 48
universalism 34
unresolved: loss 17; questions 56

validator 51
values 115
Van Gemeren 32
victim 50
viewing 105
vigil 12
virtue 49, 116
visiting hours 11
vulnerability 60, 102, 119, 149

Weedn, Flavia 41
'weeping with those who weep' 102
whirlpool 12, 151
Winston's Wish 83, 154
wisdom 51, 122, 149, 150
withdrawal 48, 50
Woodward, J. 10
wounded 15
Wright, T. 34

'You can shed tears that she is gone' 134
Young, W. P. 7

CPSIA information can be obtained at www.ICGtesting.com
Printed in the USA
LVOW071447051011

249246LV00001B/120/P